SO-AEM-648

Handwritten notes:
gift from To Ed
see Chapter 11
pp 175 - 184 by
[signature]
1991

Healing the World*

*and Me

Mark Macy, Editor

To the Future

Copyright © 1991 by Mark Macy

All rights reserved. No part of this work, except for specific sections noted in the text, may be reprinted in any form or by any means without permission in writing from the publisher.

Published by Knowledge Systems, Inc.

For a free catalog or ordering information
call (317) 241-0749 or write Knowledge Systems,
7777 West Morris Street, Indianapolis, IN 46231 USA.

Library of Congress Cataloging-in-Publication Data

Healing the world and me / Mark Macy, editor.
         p.   cm.
     Includes bibliographical references and index.
     ISBN 0-941705-16-1 : $12.95
     1. Social problems. 2. Healing--Social aspects. 3. Human
ecology. I. Macy, Mark, 1949-
HN18.H43   1990   91-14627
003--dc20   CIP

10 9 8 7 6 5 4 3 2 1

Contents

Acknowledgments

Thank God for the publication of this book! . . . three years and several iterations later than expected because of my illness and the drawn-out process of healing my life. The book (like me) is much better off because of it all. Thanks to family, friends and the early authors for your patience. I hope you all like the finished product as much as I do.

Thanks to the tremendous sources of valuable names and information available today—including International Foundation for Development Alternatives (IFDA), *New Options Newsletter,* World-Watch, Institute of Noetic Sciences, World Future Society, Institute for Soviet-American Relations (ISAR), Consortium of Peace, Research, Education and Development (COPRED), School for Esoteric Studies, Fetzer Institute, and *Transnational Perspectives*—from which many ideas and statistics and a few chapters were gleaned.

A very special thanks to Bernie Siegel, whose tremendous insights into living, loving and healing not only helped turn my life around after cancer, but also provided inspiration and a perfect christening for this book.

Thanks also to the authors of my previous anthology, *Solutions for a Troubled World*, who participated in the final chapter of this book by completing a survey of its main ideas.

Most of all, thanks to my wife Regina and son Aaron for your unconditional love.

Prologue

by Bernie Siegel, M.D.

Exploring outer space seems to hold more of a fascination for us than exploring our inner reality. We are more inclined to go out of our minds than into them. Yet if mankind had the courage to go into its own darkness and explore it, we would be much further along the path to peace and planetary healing. Just think where we would be today if all the time, money and genius spent on space exploration had been used instead to delve into the mysteries of life within us. We would certainly be enjoying a richer life with a more thorough understanding of such concepts as peace, love and healing. Curing symptoms, the broad aim of modern medicine, would take a back seat to peace of mind and genuine caring between doctor and patient. Healing patients' lives, rather than just curing their symptoms, would become the ultimate aim of medical professionals.

An inside job. Healing must begin at the most basic level. For individuals in a genuine healing mode, it means every cell in our body participates in the desire to live and love. For mankind to heal will mean every child will grow up knowing that they are loved. This pervasive love integrates life and leads to behavior on the part of cells, individuals and groups that is life-enhancing: addictions, pollution and self-destructive behavior are not practiced by truly loving people because they feel no need to seek substitutes for their love.

A healed life provides physical as well as behavioral benefits. We are, after all, a body-mind and our feelings are chemical. Messages in the form of peptide molecules are scattered throughout our bodies, concentrated in the brain, the gut and other areas, acting as a sixth sense and turning our thoughts and "gut feelings" into muscle action and growth. We are, in fact, what we think. When we feed negative or incorrect messages to our bodies via our thoughts, we are being self-destructive. On the other hand, when we laugh, love and hope, every cell in our body is aware of our happiness and we live up to our greatest potential. When we start feeding our body love, we change our pattern of thinking from *why me?* to *try me!* and life becomes a challenge and a means of expressing our love for the world.

Just as our American Indian ancestors made decisions after considering how the seventh generation succeeding them would be affected, so also will our decisions incorporate a love for others and our planet when we are genuinely healing.

A matter of choice. In order to make this love meaningful it must come of free will. This brings danger as well as meaning to the love, for if free will is involved, those who choose not to love can make life more perilous for those who do. We have the technology today to destroy the world if we do not choose to love. It is nice to believe that a miracle is about to unfold. Having witnessed many miraculous recoveries among my patients when they came to accept and give love freely, I like to envision a similar "spontaneous remission" of our planetary ills occurring in the coming years when we simply, consciously decide to choose love and healing over destruction and suffering. Meanwhile, even in this troubled age we humans are basically loving. If enough of us love we will be safe. Our loving consciousness will affect others.

For those of us who today are suffering, how can we tap into this consciousness and move in the direction of healing? The Bible and the great prophets tell us God speaks to us in dreams and visions. Regardless of our personal concept of God—the life force, the Self, DNA, a superintelligence within each of us, or whatever—the Truth as it applies to each of us can be found there. I believe that a fertilized egg contains a map to our finest personal destiny and a message that if we follow the map we can each become the best human being possible. Those individuals who learn to listen to the message become the finest people of any age. And the wonderful news is, it is a skill available to all of us. When we open to the unconscious we connect with our total knowledge and awareness and can truly find our unique path. The healing path. In healing the planet we must all learn to reconnect with our silent feelings and unconscious awareness. We must reawaken the unique clarity of vision of the child within each of us.

A subject of training. Long-term planetary healing will require that we provide this mental, emotional balance to all our growing children as well. We can begin the process by licensing parents. I say this with tongue mostly (though not entirely) in cheek. All future parents must be allowed to understand and share the difficulties of parenting and to learn ways of dealing with these difficulties, so that parents' inadequacies will not be taken out on their children.

The most serious planetary illness today is a lack of love for our children. That without love we do not grow is true literally as well as figuratively. X-rays of neglected children reveal dense lines in their bones indicating periods of no love and no growth. This disease above all others must be eliminated if we hope to achieve a peaceful, wholesome world. In the future all children will need to know three things: 1) parents do have defects, 2) age does not guarantee wisdom, and 3) all children are born loveable.

As these children are schooled, the message of love must be reaffirmed on an individual basis as well as a worldwide basis. They will learn they are children both of humankind and the universe. They will be taught that they are capable of self-healing, that they can heal themselves and their planet by their actions. They need not rely on those older than they to heal them. As this occurs, addictions and self-destructive behavior will have no place in their thinking. There will be no more Adolf Hitlers among our descendants because destruction of others will not be part of their pattern of thinking. Punishment will neither be required nor regarded as the solution to problems.

Love, the healer. This may sound like an impossibility but it is not. Unconditional love is the strongest stimulant to the immune system and the greatest healer of humankind at all levels, from individuals and families to religions and nations. When existing together with discipline, love can eliminate the need for destruction and punishment.

On a healing planet, all children will have a chance to travel widely as part of their education and see we are one family and one world. Self-interest will also mean universal interest. We will gain a sense of oneness, a knowledge that a butterfly fluttering its wings in Asia affects us in North America.

We must understand that this oneness will not come about as a response to simplistic stimuli such as threats and demands.

• What if we are threatened to change lest we all die? Fear simply brings uncertainty, weakness and illness. Transcending fear allows forgiveness of past mistakes and wrongdoings while unleashing a love that brings psychological immunity to our surroundings.

• What if we are ordered to be loving, responsible people? We will not change our behavior if it does not change how we feel about living.

We sometimes think the world would be a nicer place if other people were more like us, other cultures more like our own. We must keep in mind that we cannot change another person or another culture, only ourself and our own. But we *can* almost magically create the other person (or culture) by what we are like. Changing ourself changes those around us without trying to mold them in our own image.

Changes which lead to our enjoying life more fully do not seem like work or sacrifice, and they are incorporated smoothly into our behavior patterns. *All* of my patients who make a transition from suffering and dying to peace of mind and healing have made an enormous change to a loving, accepting attitude. Changing our mind often requires listening to our heart. That sums up the future of medicine as well as the future of our planet.

We should keep in mind that we can't cure everything. We will never feed all the hungry, house all the homeless, or end all epidemics. But we as family members, friends and medical professionals *can* care for everyone and for the planet. It is through caring that genuine healing can occur. Healing of our spirit, our self, and our life.

When we create a loving consciousness on the planet with a generation of loved children, the change in behavior will be a part of living. No one will feel that they are giving up anything or working harder. They will do it because it feels right to live that way. The by-product will be a healed planet filled with healed human beings created by a loving, healing consciousness that unites all living matter.

Dr. Bernie Siegel is the author of
Peace, Love and Healing and
Love, Medicine and Miracles

Introduction

I'm wrapping up this book during a period of seclusion among the giant redwoods in the national park around Klamath, California. Two of my favorite things have always been coasts and lush forests, both easily accessible from here. The path from my back door leads into a redwood forest a hundred yards away. There are coastal trailheads down the road a mile or so in either direction. If you come here in the quiet months between tourist season and fishing season the area can be quite peaceful, although the frequent appearance of logging trucks roaring along the winding highway among the noble giants, hauling load after load of their dead cousins, can be a bit unsettling. A major issue today is the alarming rate of destruction of the equatorial rain forests, while the rain forests in the US are disappearing even faster.

Over the years I've taken many such excursions into the woods, spending several days or weeks or months getting retuned to Nature and self through meditation, contemplation, running, writing, and music.

There are differences this time, though, the main one being that I now have a wife (Regina) and son (Aaron). Having a loving family waiting for me is like having a treasure at the end of the rainbow. Warm human bonds are a fundamental human need which can enhance the healing of self, society and planet, as attested by several authors of this book, especially Paul Wachtel, Judith Clabes, Majid Rahnema, Robert Muller and Hazel Henderson.

Another unique aspect of this trip is the fact that I'm healing from cancer that was diagnosed in 1988, hence this book's underlying theme of healing. I'm still recovering from the effects of my illness during an era when the world is in need of healing from its own serious illnesses—international tensions, environmental destruction, dwindling resources, widespread poverty and hunger—subjects of the final chapters of this book.

The question that sticks in the minds of most cancer patients is, "Why did it happen to me?" I have spent the past two years soul-searching, reading, researching, and talking to other cancer patients. My conclusion: it obviously goes deeper than the malignant tumor.

Typically a living system like the body (or like the biosphere blanketing our planet, for that matter) can absorb a lot of stress and toxicity before showing serious symptoms. By then there is so much sickness built up in the system that will take a great deal of time and effort to heal. Symptoms are likely to persist long after causes have been removed. A person who toxifies his or her body during many years of poor eating habits—sweets, high-fat foods, alcohol and coffee—and begins to follow a wholesome, cleansing diet, can expect toxins to have been built up in the tissues and cells to the point where it will take several months for the blood, three or four years for the organs and soft tissues, and seven years for the bones to be completely rejuvenated and rebuilt. So, all told, it can take about seven years for the body to clean and rebuild itself.

A massive life form like the global ecosystem will no doubt need substantially longer than seven years to regain balance from the stresses that are now showing up as erratic weather patterns, spreading deserts, and dying seas, lakes and rivers. But even these are just early symptoms. More serious ones are probably coming. During global warming, for example, the oceans warm slowly (consider how long it takes a pot of water to start boiling on a stove!) so that the things we are doing today to promote global warming will not be fully felt for some 25 years in the northern hemisphere, 60 years in the south.

Wouldn't it be nice if there were some force or substance or a magic potion that we could apply to our bodies and minds, our societies and our planet, to help bring things into balance, bringing us contentment and bliss, social stability and world peace? Not just a drug to numb the nerves and promote more serious imbalances, but a genuine mind-body, head-heart balancer that would boil over into our groups and spread around the world.

It seems that there is such a force that goes by a variety of names. In the western world its sensations are often called love, grace or bliss, while the force itself is called life energy, the life force, or the holy spirit. In traditional Chinese medicine the force is called Qi (pronounced "chee"). In Chinese religion it is called Tao. In India's yoga community it is called shakti or kundalini.

When we feel that force flowing through our bodies and minds in a balanced, unobstructed fashion, we know we are in a healing mode. Our immune system grows stronger. Gradually we gravitate toward more wholesome foods. We start moving more fluidly, avoiding life's bumps and bruises—the emotional ones as well as the physical ones. We become happier and healthier. Our love boils over into our social groups and things get better all around us.

It is when we delve lovelessly inward into our microcosm of cells and molecules or when we explore lovelessly outward into the puzzling contradictions of society to analyze, dissect and measure, that healing becomes a complex issue. When we stay "right here" in the familiar world and tap into the forces available to us, life can become an utter joy in all its simplicity and beauty.

While we can help heal society by opening our mind to knowledge, we must also heal ourself by opening our heart to love.

Nonetheless, we should not be too blasé regarding the task ahead of us. "The Biblical ten plagues of Egypt and the deluge will seem mild in comparison to what can happen if we do not act now," the Brundtland Report* concludes. I have no doubt that if

---

* Note: Throughout this book are scattered mentions of the Brundtland Report, a nickname for the report by the UN-appointed World Commission on Environment and Development (WCED). Formally titled *Our Common Future*, the Brundtland Report was published by Oxford University in 1987 and is available in most libraries. The WCED was formed by the UN in 1984 to assess the troubles facing our environment, and to set a sensible course for future development by getting nations to work together, and raising global awareness and commitment at all levels of world society. In 1987 the commission completed its global study. This, in a nutshell, is what they found:

The primary goal of all nations collectively and individually must be to revive economic growth in a way that is sustainable and fair, and promotes security. Sustainability means that countries will be at peace with the

we accept today's crises as opportunities rather than catastrophes we can pre-empt the brunt of the coming storm.

As you dig into the book, keep in mind that it is not intended as a complete package of solutions to the challenges we face today, but a sampling of ideas from around the globe that would help us heal ourselves at the personal, social and planetary levels, especially when combined with the ideas presented by the authors of my previous anthology, *Solutions for a Troubled World.*

—*Mark Macy*

---

environment. With fairness they will be at peace with each other, and with security they will be at peace with themselves.

The commission members didn't solve all the world's problems, but they certainly explored deeply, established a framework, and fired up individuals to take further steps. The dedication of the commission members—particularly their chairwoman, Dr. Gro Harlem Brundtland (who is also the prime minister of Norway and is being discussed as a likely next secretary general of the UN) and the success of their efforts will undoubtedly reserve a spot for them in our grandchildren's history books as genuine, turn-of-the-century heroes.

Part I:
Healing Our Lives

Life is an infinitely complex chain of system nests. A person, for example, contains several major biological subsystems for such processes as digestion, circulation and intercellular communication. These are, in turn, composed of organs and tissues, which are composed of cells which are composed of organelles, downward. . . inward, perhaps, to infinity.

At the same time, a person is part of several social groups, including perhaps family, workplace, professional organizations, clubs and friendships. These in turn may compose larger social groups. Family is part of a neighborhood. A company may be part of an international industry or chain of businesses. Neighborhoods might be part of a city. A city is part of a nation. A nation is part of humanity, and is also part of an ecosystem in which it is growing. The political borders on a map do not surround a nation; not really. They really surround a large chunk of the global ecosystem on which a nation happens to be growing. Cities and farms, highways and other organs and tissues of the actual nation speckle the global landscape like patches of mold on an old peach.

Life is an infinitely complex tapestry of nested systems.

To get a proper perspective on healing, we need to forget the notion of dissecting one of those systems from the tapestry and studying it by itself. Instead, we need to zoom in on a segment of tapestry, explore the smaller subsystems within the system we're looking at, and also observe the larger systems into which the system fits.

Healing implies that something within that tapestry is out of balance. Systems are not fitting together as they should be. Healing is the process of getting back into balance. Healing individuals are those whose internal organs, tissues and cells are becoming increasingly integrated, functioning together more smoothly. Mind and body are working together well. The head and the heart are finding a gentle balance of logic and emotion, rational thought and intuition.

While that is all happening inside, big changes are occurring outside too. The healing individuals are starting to interact more smoothly with the systems they are part of. Conflicts and communication barriers within the family dissolve, so that the family functions better. There may emerge a growing fondness for one's job and for the people one works with, greater acceptance and tolerance for individuals whom the healing individual once found distasteful. Friendships become closer. Trust and love become a binding force between the healing individual and society. In Part One of this book:

David Eisenberg, M.D. takes a fascinating look at the force or energy of life which courses through our bodies, integrating the living structures within us. Westerners are starting to pay attention to this force which has played a major role in Chinese healing for centuries.

Emmett Miller, M.D. takes us on a healing journey of the mind. Visualization techniques can play an important part in healing our bodies and, perhaps, our planet by helping us function more smoothly and lovingly inside and out.

Mark Macy, editor, describes the healing changes in his life after a bout with cancer in 1988—changes within him and in his dealings with others that shaped the course of this book.

Judith Clabes shows how healthy, happy individuals are the products of families manifesting abundant love, care, trust, discipline and commitment. Many families today are in need of healing.

Chapter One:
Energy Medicine in China

by David Eisenberg, M.D.

His background. Instructor in Medicine, Harvard Medical School; Associate in Medicine, Beth Israel Hospital, Boston. Author of *Encounters with Qi: Exploring Chinese Medicine*.

His chapter. A brief history of Chinese medicine and its growing interest in the West since the early 1970s. Energy medicine (Qi Gong), acupuncture, acupressure and herbal medicine all could be valuable assets to conventional Western medical procedures if properly researched and validated. A strategy for undertaking such validation is laid out.

Without prospective randomized trials producing convincing data, so-called energy medicine will not be accepted by mainstream health-care providers.

Energy Medicine in China

by David Eisenberg, M.D.

Vine Deloria, writing about the evolution of medical systems prior to the one currently in use, made the following observation: "For primitive people the presence of energy and power is the starting point of their analysis and understanding of the natural world ... primitive people felt power but did not measure it. Today we measure power but are not able to feel it."

Rene Dubos, commenting on modern scientific principles, has reminded us that: "Sometimes the more measurable drives out the most important."

Researchers of so-called energy medicine are a curious lot. We unearth ancient practices, dust them off, clean them with modern solvents and study them under the lens of high technology. All the while, we seek to distill simple truths about health and illness.

Traditional Chinese Medicine

China is a nation of 1.1 billion people where more than 800 million people reside in rural areas. These individuals lead a lifestyle not altogether different from the lifestyles of their parents, grandparents and distant ancestors.

It is said of rural China that the three greatest changes in the past century are the introduction of the bicycle, of the thermos bottle and, most recently, the absence of war for more than a quarter century. Chinese customs have changed relatively little. Children, in the eyes of the Chinese people, remain the most precious gift of nature and the source of hope for future generations. But a Chinese child growing up in the latter portion of the twentieth century will surely face tumultuous change. By law, a Chinese family can have only one child. As such, an entire generation of Chinese children will grow up without an understanding of what it means to have brothers and sisters. Moreover, Chinese children will witness a rapidly changing economy and a volatile political atmosphere—one which is struggling to embrace democracy and Western attitudes without destroying its own cultural heritage.

Furthermore, Chinese children growing up in the 1990s will live in a country where there are two distinct systems of medical care. One system, traditional Chinese medicine, is likely favored by the children's grandparents and rural neighbors. The other system, which we refer to as "modern Western medicine," is likely preferred by the parents, educated relatives and urban neighbors.

Traditional Chinese medicine evolved over two thousand years under the influence of Buddhist and Taoist priests. This medical system emerged in isolation from Western science as we know it. Not until the middle of the nineteenth century were principles of the scientific method introduced to China. This occurred as a result of education offered by medical missionaries from Europe and the United States.

By the turn of the century American and European missionaries had established medical clinics, hospitals, and several medical schools on the Chinese mainland. Prominent professors from universities such as Harvard, Yale, and Johns Hopkins lectured at the newly created Chinese medical schools.

Western medicine became extremely popular with China's intellectuals and with its governmental leaders. In an effort to promote Western medicine the Nationalist Government in the 1920s went so far as to outlaw traditional Chinese medicine on the grounds that it was "backwards and superstitious." This effort failed, as the Chinese people perceived Western medicine to be alien, crude, and highly unnatural.

In 1950, following the establishment of the People's Republic of China, Chairman Mao Tse-tung was faced with a political dilemma: There were approximately 500 million people in China but only 38,000 Western-style medical doctors. At the same time, however, there were approximately 500,000 traditionally trained Chinese doctors. Understandably, Chairman Mao launched a political campaign to "unite medical workers young and old of the traditional and Western schools to organize a solid front." For the past four decades this call for unity and integration has persisted in the People's Republic of China.

However, if one reviews statistics from the Chinese Ministry of Health regarding medical manpower throughout the People's Republic of China today, it is clear that over the past three decades the pendulum has shifted from traditional medicine to modern Western medicine. Today Western-style physicians outnumber traditionally trained medical doctors six to one and Western-style hospital beds outnumber those in traditional Chinese hospitals by thirteen to one. This trend toward a dominance of modern Western medicine will continue for the foreseeable future.

Its Introduction to the West

What about the introduction of traditional Chinese medicine to the West? In the United States the turning point, I believe, was a single newspaper article written by James Reston, a prominent journalist from *The New York Times*.

In 1971, while accompanying the Nixon-Kissinger entourage, James Reston wrote an article entitled "Now Let Me Tell You About My Appendectomy In Peking." Reston developed acute appendicitis while visiting Beijing and was operated on using Western anesthesia. The surgery was uneventful; however, he suffered profound postoperative pain in the area of his incision. The Chinese medical authorities summoned two prominent acupuncturists to treat these symptoms. Their treatment consisted of inserting several needles. So prompt and complete was Reston's pain relief, that he could barely contain himself from describing this curious technique in detail. This description introduced the West to a therapy which the Chinese referred to as "acupuncture anesthesia."

James Reston's article triggered an enormous surge of interest in this therapy. Medical teams composed of experts traveled to China to witness surgical procedures involving it. Many of these experts returned to the United States utterly convinced that acupuncture anesthesia was a real phenomenon, not merely hypnosis or sham.

I was a college freshman at that time and elected to do an independent study project regarding acupuncture anesthesia.

Little did I know that none of the 100 libraries at Harvard University contained a single page describing it.

Acupuncture had been used to treat common illnesses for more than 2,000 years; however, its application as a surgical anesthetic was new. This had to do with the fact that there was no major surgery in traditional Chinese medicine. Major surgery was considered to be a mutilation of the body and the body was considered to be the ultimate gift of one's parents. Filial piety dictated that one never deface the ultimate gift of one's ancestors. Therefore, there was no major surgery in China—only the sewing up of superficial wounds and stabilization of bone fractures.

Acupuncture was not applied to the surgical amphitheater until the late 1950s, as a direct consequence of Chairman Mao's political directive that physicians from Chinese and Western backgrounds work together to "form a united front."

In 1972, when I became interested in acupuncture, there were no English translations of Chinese experimental texts dealing with acupuncture as an anesthetic. Instead, I stumbled on English translations of famous reference texts of traditional Chinese medicine. Chief among them was a book entitled *The Yellow Emperor's Canon of Internal Medicine*. Following is a passage from that book:

> To administer medicine to diseases which have already developed and thereby suppress bodily chaos which has already occurred is comparable to the behavior of those who would begin to dig a well after they have grown thirsty, or those who would begin to cast weapons after they have engaged in battle. Would these actions not be too late?. . .
>
> I have heard that in early times the people lived to be over 100 years old. But these days people reach only half that age and must curtail their activities. Does the world change from generation to generation or does man become negligent of the laws of nature?. . .
>
> Today people do not know how to find contentment within. They are not skilled in the control of their spirits. For these reasons they reach only half of their 100 years and then they degenerate.

The Canon of Internal Medicine is still used today as the primary reference for traditional Chinese medicine.

This ancient text helped me understand the basic theoretical differences which distinguish Chinese (that is, Oriental) medical systems from those used today in the West. Specifically, traditional Chinese medicine emphasized prevention over intervention. It also emphasized that one's lifestyle, including diet, exercise, thoughts, and emotions, plays a critical role in the natural course of illness and one's ability to maintain health.

I was intrigued by the basic principles of Chinese medicine and set out to learn the Chinese language in the hope that some day I could study both traditional Chinese and modern Western medicine.

In 1979, when I was a fourth-year medical student at Harvard Medical School, the United States normalized relations with the People's Republic of China. The National Academy of Sciences selected me to serve as the first US medical exchange student to China. In 1979 and 1980, I studied Chinese medicine at the Beijing College of Traditional Chinese Medicine.

Toward Complete Healing

We sometimes unconsciously regard sickness as the norm and healing as the goal, which should not be the case in life. Most living systems, whether human bodies or social systems, remain stable by staying in a constant state of repair and maintenance. As parts weaken with age and use (whether cells and tissues in the body or roads and buildings in society) they are repaired or replaced, and the system thrives. When individuals and groups start behaving in a way that is harmful to the system around them (whether germs and tumors in the body or criminals and organized crime in society), they are removed from the system and, again, the system thrives. This is all part of the day-to-day clean-up operation of a living system. It is only when the system is weakened by stress and wrong nourishment that the repair and maintenance abilities wind down and the system gradually loses its ability to deal with those who would by their actions harm it.

Perhaps the most important prerequisite for a healthy system is knowledge distributed to all members. This certainly seems to be true of societies and the world at large. Recent findings indicate that it is true of biosystems like the human body as well; knowledge needs to be dispersed to all the members. In *Quantum Healing* (Bantam, 1989), author Deepak Chopra M.D. describes how intelligence is not something centralized in the brain as is so often regarded today. Rather, it is spread infinitely throughout life at all levels. All the DNA molecules in all the cells of every person, plant and animal on the globe share the same

I was not prepared for the education I received in Beijing. Without realizing it at the time, I was receiving my initial formal education in "energy medicine."

I was fascinated by the principal methods of physical diagnosis: tongue and pulse examination. It was hard to imagine that each radial artery could be successfully palpated in six separate locations (three superficial and three deep) and that a masterful clinician could differentiate among 40 different pulse variations at each of the twelve pulse points. More spectacular still was the claim that these subtle pulse variations enabled the clinician to know with accuracy the etiology and extent of the patient's pathology within specific internal organs. Such correlations were unknown to me.

More peculiar still was the Chinese diagnostic approach using the tongue. Students of traditional Chinese medicine were required to master several hundred tongue variations. The size, color,

---

eternal knowledge of life. It is this knowledge spread to all 10 trillion cells of the body, more than anything else, that keeps the body well-integrated and healthy. Dr. Chopra describes what happens when knowledge is not well dispersed:

"When consciousness is fragmented, it starts a war in the mind-body system. This war lies behind many diseases. . . . The conflict is being waged "in here," contrary to the germ theory of disease, which tries to tell us that the war was started "out there" by invaders of every kind. For every time that you actually have to fight off a disease by getting sick, there are dozens, if not hundreds, of times when your body has warded off sickness without any overt symptoms. It is only when there is a distortion "in here" that the immune system loses its ability to silently defend, heal and remember."

The same holds true for social systems and humanity at large. Societies often blame other societies for their problems when in fact it is imbalances and conditions within society that are making life difficult. It's easier, for example, for the US in the 1990s to blame its drug problem on its Third World, southern neighbors (where the drugs come from) than to uncover and heal its own internal weaknesses that make society vulnerable to drugs, such factors as weakened family ties, lost sense of community, shortcomings in education, and waning spirituality.

Dr. Chopra writes near the end of his book: "The vital issue is not how to win the war but how to keep the peace in the first place."

Unfortunately, many individuals and societies today must regain their lost sense of inner peace first.

—MHM

coating, tooth indentation, etc., of each tongue type was said to enable the clinican to make a specific diagnosis in terms of location and etiology of pathology. Again this claim seemed utterly fantastic and new to me.

Not only were the diagnostic approaches to the physical examination alien, so were the specific therapeutic interventions within traditional Chinese medical hospitals. Each, I came to learn, was based on an "energy" system.

Treatment

Acupuncture, for example, known in the West primarily in regard to surgical analgesia, was used daily in the treatment of almost every medical, surgical and psychiatric illness known. Its application as a means of "restoring energy balance" was yet another new observation for me. Clinicians spoke of "putting energy through the needles" and "taking energy out of the body" in a language which was alien to me.

Acupressure massage, based on a system of points and meridians identical to acupuncture, was yet another unexplored modality. Again, claims of energy transfer were used by my mentors in describing what they were doing in diagnosing and treating patients on the massage table. I was impressed clinically by the extent to which patients with acute musculoskeletal pain and/or pain in association with chronic neurologic or musculoskeletal problems found relief from massage therapy. More importantly, in many instances patients' relief was not short-lived but, rather, lasted for days, weeks or months in a fashion which I could not explain. These were among my most humbling observations.

Herbal medicine, not acupressure or acupuncture, is the principal mode of Chinese intervention. Over the past two millennia the Chinese have developed a vast pharmacopoeia of plant, animal and mineral substances based on empirical observation and clinical experience.

Herbal therapy is unquestionably the most respected and difficult of all Chinese interventions because it requires the study of hundreds of herbal preparations used in complicated combinations specifically for the purpose of rebalancing bodily excess, deficiency or stagnation. Without a mastery of classical Chinese language, pulse and tongue diagnosis and insight into

Chinese pathophysiology, herbal therapy is a foreboding if not impossible discipline.

Qi Gong. The other Chinese medical therapy which is most closely related to the notion of Western "energy healing" is that of Qi Gong (pronounced "chee gong").

Qi Gong is a martial art, arguably the oldest and most important martial art, from which other forms of martial arts have evolved. The physical movements of Qi Gong, which are circular, symmetrical, and slow, are similar to those movements used in other martial arts (such as Tai Chi Chuan and Kung Fu). In addition to the physical movements, the practitioner is instructed in the art of centering, of achieving a particular state of physical balance, and, simultaneously, to meditate.

The practice of Qi Gong involves some of the key elements found in Western relaxation training. These include paying attention to one's breathing, establishing a passive disregard toward one's thoughts, and—unique to Qi Gong—instructions in techniques to sense the source of one's Qi (vital energy) at a point below the navel and to learn to move it through one's body. I will return to this unusual aspect of Qi Gong.

It is said that anyone can learn Qi Gong exercises and that it takes approximately three to six months before one can "feel one's Qi" (in the form of heat or fullness) and begin to move it at will.

The practice of Qi Gong, when analyzed from a Western perspective, may be thought of as a combination of behavioral techniques. These are typically performed for 30 to 60 minutes every day of the year. The behavioral components of Qi Gong include the elicitation of the relaxation response and/or other aspects of relaxation training, aerobic exercise, progressive muscular relaxation, guided imagery, and elements of the placebo effect. In China, where an estimated *50 million* persons practice Qi Gong every day, there is an unprecedented opportunity to investigate the impact of behavioral (that is, non-pharmacologic, cognitive) therapies as they relate to a multitude of illnesses.

The Concept of Qi

There is a single fundamental concept of traditional Chinese medicine which helps clarify the seemingly disparate diagnostic and therapeutic techniques I have summarized. This concept is called "Qi" (vital energy).

"Qi" is said to be that which differentiates animate from inanimate. The body is viewed as a complicated series of conduits through which Qi flows. These conduits are the acupuncture meridians referred to in Chinese diagrams depicting human anatomy. Pathogenesis relates to the excess or deficiency inextricably linked to the force of Yin ("female," "cold," "hollow," etc.) and its opposing force, Yang ("male," "hot," "solid," etc.).

The Chinese clinician's task is to identify where the Qi exists in excess or is deficient. This is done chiefly by means of taking a history, observing and using pulse and tongue diagnosis. The diagnostic label used by the Chinese clinician refers to the specific imbalance which has been noted on physical examination. Each therapy, whether it includes needles, herbs, changes in diet or meditation, is aimed at reestablishing the balance of Qi.

There is one more piece of traditional Chinese terminology which is worth mentioning. "Internal Qi Gong" or "Soft Qi Gong" refers to an individual's ability to sense and move his/her own Qi within his/her own body. "External Qi Gong" or "Hard Qi Gong" refers to the (alleged) ability of some Qi Gong practitioners to emit their Qi externally so as to influence other animate or inanimate structures.

The notion of emitting energy from the human body is yet another example of how traditional Chinese medical thought diverges radically from that of conventional Western medicine. Traditional Chinese medicine asserts that Qi Gong masters can emit Qi at will and use this energy as a treatment for common illness.

The notion of "Qi" is not unique to China. It is found within the medical systems of Tibet, India, ancient Greece, branches of the Catholic Church, and also has similarities to more recent theories such as that of "animal magnetism" proposed by Mesmer in the eighteenth century.

In the late 1970s and early 1980s the masters of Qi Gong reemerged and began to perform publicly throughout China. They had all "gone underground" during the 1960s and '70s as a result of the cultural revolution's ban on Qi Gong (which was labeled "superstition" by China's political authorities). These individuals claimed to have practiced Qi Gong from early childhood and proudly displayed their seemingly supernatural skills to audiences as large as 50,000 persons. Qi Gong masters split stones with their hands and their foreheads, had trucks drive over them, had massive stone slabs lowered on their bodies by cranes, claimed to be able to see within human bodies and to move inanimate objects at will. The claims seemed carnival-like and appeared to be well-rehearsed circus acts.

Researching Qi Gong

My personal interest in Qi Gong was sparked as a result of a television broadcast in 1980 which suggested that scientific laboratories in Beijing and Shanghai were applying rigorous methods of investigation to the physiologic changes produced by Qi Gong masters. First among these observations were reports of thermal change in surface skin measurements of Qi Gong masters who were "emitting Qi." Thermally sensitive films suggested that when Qi Gong masters emitted energy, the energy tracked down lines in the forearms and legs which were similar to classical acupuncture meridians.

A second series of publications in the area of microbiology were more fantastic still. Professor Feng Li Da of Beijing published an article pertaining to the predictable change of bacterial cell growth in response to external Qi emission by Qi Gong masters. Her paper reported on the ability of several Qi Gong masters to increase or decrease bacterial cell growth in a variety of common bacteria. Dr. Feng claimed to have replicated these experiments on numerous occasions in multiple laboratory settings and seemed confident of her results.

A more recent series of assertions has to do with the claim that certain Qi Gong masters can modulate AC electrical current from any common wall socket and act as a "human rheostat."

After attending a conference in Beijing in October 1988 I was asked by a Qi Gong master if he could demonstrate his skill to me on a visit to my hotel room. He came equipped with an electrical volt meter and a simple wiring device. The device was no more than a plug attached to two wires with live ends. He put the plug in the wall and demonstrated its current by lighting lightbulbs and then tested the current on his hand-carried volt meter. He then licked his thumb and forefinger of both hands and grasped the two live wires. I was horrified and worried he would quickly be electrocuted before me. He was not. Moreover, he convinced me that he could light a lightbulb by touching it with other fingers from both hands. More curious still was his ability to regulate voltage across his two hands, at will, simply by touching the volt meter with the ground in one hand, the meter device in the other. On several attempts he regulated the voltage from 0 to 220 volts, or held the voltage constant, at will, upon my request.

Because I have grown increasingly skeptical of such provocative claims, I asked him how I could be certain he was in fact conducting electricity and not simply fooling me by means of some extraordinary high technology trick. He offered to touch me with his hands while he was connected to the wall socket. I declined, but a colleague with me at the time volunteered. When touched on the shoulder by the Qi Gong master, my colleague's trapezius and biceps muscles went into spasm. Moreover, the Qi Gong master could control the electrical current so as to induce the spasm or not. I allowed the Qi Gong master to touch me for a split second, long enough to feel the live current emanating from his forefinger. He was "live" all right.

In a final demonstration the Qi Gong master took two metal skewers along with a one-pound pork steak which he had brought with him. He put the two skewers through the steak then grabbed the skewers, one in the left hand and one in the right so as to complete an electrical circuit. Having grasped the wires along with the two skewers the circuit was engaged and the pork chop began to smoke and flame. Within minutes there was a medium-well-done pork chop which my Qi Gong friend sliced and offered to serve! I was astounded by this demonstration and have no adequate explanation for why the Qi Gong master did not injure his skin, or cause a serious heart irregularity, seizure or other damage to his own person.

Such feats are no more than a tantalizing introduction to the many provocative clinical applications of so-called External Qi therapy. For example, Lin Ho Sheng, Qi Gong master in Shanghai, claims to have emitted Qi directly to the acupuncture points used for acupuncture anesthesia. As reported, this type of Qi Gong anesthesia was successfully used in several dozen operations involving the thyroid gland or abdomen. There is no explanation for this kind of claim. Hypnosis has been flatly denied by the

Chinese. I am unaware of any replication of this kind of analgesic technique outside of Shanghai.

Qi Gong masters throughout traditional Chinese medical colleges in the People's Republic of China are using External Qi Gong as a treatment for a wide variety of illnesses. They typically treat patients with chronic neurologic and musculoskeletal disease, including multiple sclerosis.

More spectacular still is the observation that large numbers of patients said to have biopsy-proven, non-malignant cancer are being treated with a combination of Internal and External Qi Gong therapy. Hundreds of purported cancer patients meet at dawn each morning for the purpose of practicing Internal Qi Gong and receiving External Qi Gong therapy from a Qi Gong master. Moreover, the Chinese lay press frequently displays headlines such as: "Qi Gong Defeats Breast Cancer." These articles tend to summarize anecdotal case histories and are rarely if ever substantiated in medical journals.

I wish to point out that recent estimates suggested that 50-60 million Chinese practice Qi Gong at dawn each day for the purpose of disease prevention or in an attempt to alter the natural course of serious or lethal illness.

A Proposed Research Strategy

I would like to offer a strategy for experimental validation of assertions regarding Chinese energy medicine. First, the assertions:

1. "Qi" (vital energy) exists as a physical entity. The Chinese claim the Qi can be measured, controlled and has biological and clinical significance.

2. "Qi meridians" (energy fields) exist as physical entities. The Chinese claim that meridians are measurable, and necessary for pulse, tongue and energy diagnosis. Furthermore, Chinese theory suggests that meridians can be predictably influenced by acupuncture stimulation, herbal therapies, massage, Qi Gong or other cognitive interventions.

3. Tongue, pulse and energy diagnoses are reliable and may help to elucidate important physiologic relationships. The Chinese claim that subtle variations noted on their radial artery, the tongue and along acupuncture meridians can elucidate the location and severity of internal organ pathology.

4. Internal and/or external manipulation of "Qi" can alter the natural course of illness. The Chinese specifically assert that Qi Gong therapy can alter illness patterns in malignant cancers, chronic obstructive pulmonary disease, arthritis, etc.) psychiatric disorders (such as anxiety, depression and schizophrenia) and immuno–deficiency (for example, AIDS).

5. Paranormal (that is, psychic) abilities are "Qi related" phenomena. There is a long-held Chinese claim that individuals who practice and become masterful at manipulating internal or external Qi are capable of unique paranormal skills.

Now, a proposed strategy:

• My opinion is that we should emphasize basic science experiments before attempting to design and implement clinical trials involving human subjects. My rationale for this is based, in part, on the fact that clinical subjects committees in hospital and academic institutions are unlikely to approve human subjects experiments if they have insufficient basic science data to support their objectives.

• A specific list of basic science experiments pertaining to energy medicine should include demonstrations of the effects of Qi on a variety of electromagnetic fields, bacterial growth patterns, cell and tissue culture models, and plant and animal physiology. Without measurable, predictable and reproducible evidence in these areas, clinical research will be difficult if not impossible to promote.

• With regard to clinical investigations, the first category is that of diagnosis. An effort should be made to assess, in a critical fashion, the diagnostic acumen of "gifted healers." They should be tested in comparison to the diagnostic acumen of modern technology. Moreover, there should be an attempt to describe inter-rater reliability as well as test-retest reliability among so-called "Energy Diagnosticians."

• The same general philosophy should ideally be applied to devices and machines which claim to be based on "subtle energy" mechanisms. These should all be subject to controlled study in a rigorous fashion.

• A separate set of experiments should ideally assess the ability of healers and/or energy devices to induce *acute* physiologic change in human subjects. For instance, can healers or "energy devices" predictably alter organ function (for example, renal flow or cardiac output) in a fashion which is safe and reliable?

Once demonstrations of acute physiologic change are completed, experiments should be designed to document *sustained* physiologic change. Claims of altering the natural course of illness will likely only be accepted if and when evidence of sustained physiologic change can be supplied.

• If clinical therapeutic trials are to be implemented, they will need to meet rigorous clinical epidemiologic criteria in order to demonstrate efficacy and effectiveness. Ideally, such studies should avoid anecdotes and case studies in favor of randomized controlled trials. Designing such trials will be challenging in that they will need to include non-biased patient populations, controls for confounding variables (such as co-intervention, contamination, experimental bias, etc.). The confounder which is most apt to cause methodological difficulty is that of expectancy of relief (for example, placebo effect). Without careful assessment of expectancy factors prior to, during and post intervention, these studies will likely be subject to savage criticism. Statistical methods will need to include meticulous sample-size calculations and attention to both statistical and clinical significance.

• If and when clinical trials involving therapeutic modalities such as acupuncture, herbal medicine, energy emission devices and/or Qi Gong are implemented, these trials will likely need to involve multiple centers, hundreds of patients followed over months or years and strict outcome parameters which include objective variables such as health costs, days of work lost and overall medical expenses. Such studies may require the professional involvement of dozens of skilled researchers and will likely cost hundreds of thousand or millions of dollars to complete. Without prospective randomized trials producing convincing clinical data collected under rigorously controlled conditions, so-called energy medicine will not likely be accepted or promoted by mainstream health care providers and third-party insurers.

Utilizing Constructive Criticism

I have a number of suggestions whereby energy medicine researchers can work together to build credibility by inviting constructive criticism from qualified skeptical colleagues.

The first priority might be to create professional forums wherein debate pertaining to energy medicine basic science and clinical investigations can take place. Such debates may take the form of prioritizing research projects, the utilization of financial resources, popularization of ongoing research and a more meticulous review of work in progress.

We should consider identifying and electing appropriate experts to serve as mentors and scientific advisers with regard to energy medicine research. Such individuals might offer constructive criticism to protocols prior to their implementation. Once successfully implemented, this mentor (or scientific advisory) group could assist in refining data analyses and perhaps attempt to implement a replication of successful experiments in the laboratories of qualified skeptical colleagues.

Ideally, if experiments can be critiqued and replicated in the laboratories of critical colleagues, they would stand a far greater chance of being accepted in peer-reviewed journals. Moreover, having engaged qualified skeptical scientists prior to publication, professional criticism post-publication is apt to be predictable and more easily handled. This group might also consider a formal pledge to avoid public disclosure of critical experiments and/or manuscripts prior to acceptance for publication in peer-reviewed journals.

Last, scientists investigating energy medicine-related phenomena should be encouraged to share and publish experiments which have resulted in negative findings as well as those with positive results. Only in this way will the field gain credibility and will researchers be properly informed so as to avoid nonproductive methods of inquiry.

I conclude my remarks with a Chinese proverb: "Real gold does not fear the heat of even the hottest fire." Qi and Qi-related phenomena, if real, are like precious gold. Undoubtedly, once subjected to the heat of criticism, they will be reshaped and recast, but not destroyed. This process of enrichment will enable investigators to demonstrate more clearly the value of "energy"-related biological phenomena.

From a paper presented at the John E. Fetzer Foundation Conference: "Energy Fields, Meridians, Chi and Device Technology" May 11-14, 1989; and subsequently published in *Noetic Sciences Review*, Spring 1990. Reprinted with permissions.

Chapter Two:
A Vision of Peace

by Emmett Miller, M.D.

His background. A holistic physician and organizational consultant by profession, a poet and musician at heart, he has been a major force in bringing systems thinking and humanistic psychology to medicine since the late 1960s. A pioneer in the use of audio tapes for relaxation, guided imagery and wellness. Offers patients self-care techniques to bring balance and health to mind, body, heart and spirit. Gives seminars on personal motivation, achievement and excellence.

His chapter. This chapter guides us into a rich, green forest, along a winding path to a mountaintop, and upward into the quiet peace of space. Confronted by obstacles and driven by commitment and inspiration, we are really journeying within ourselves. When fed into our subconscious minds during meditation, these vivid ideas become more than a story. Miracles are written between the lines.

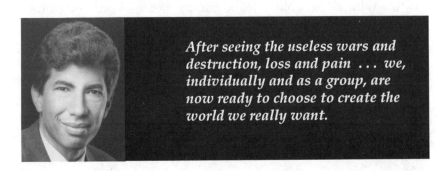

After seeing the useless wars and destruction, loss and pain ... we, individually and as a group, are now ready to choose to create the world we really want.

A Vision of Peace

by Emmett Miller, M.D.

In the booming, buzzing confusion of making and doing, of working and planning, hurrying and worrying, of traffic jams and people jams, sometimes a gentle voice within whispers, "Stop. Stop the noise, the striving, the incessant doing. Turn away from the stress and the hurry. Give yourself a moment of peace."

Right now, become aware that if you wish, you can choose, for a few minutes, to let go of all thoughts of the present and of the past, that you can focus your awareness within and further evolve your vision of the future you would like to create.

1:00

Sense within yourself that the sky is no longer a limit, for you have the freedom to choose. Whether you choose to influence the world around you or to focus on your own personal development, you are capable of imagining and choosing to accomplish anything, even things no one has ever before attempted or even believed to be possible. As you set your goal and commit to it, you awaken within the ability to be the master of your own inner universe.

(A Personal Vision)

Now, while deeply relaxed, find in your mind a special place in this emerging world where you can be alone with your goals and your vision. Imagine a forest path leading to a springtime meadow that is yours and yours alone.

You reach a river and a rainbow bridge, and cross it effortlessly, with a single, powerful stride. And as you **2:00** look around at the lovely surroundings you feel at home here in your special place . . . your beautiful garden. Soft fragrances greeting you with each step. Luminous colors sparkling in the sunlight. You notice the flowers around you gently swaying on the breeze, the birds and small squirrels busy and active, and the colors deep and rich . . . a sense of everything being fresh and young in this springtime meadow.

And only a few short steps away you discover a crystal pool and the bubbling, swirling water of a mountain spring. And here you allow yourself to rest **3:00** with your back firmly supported by a wise, old tree. Softly gazing at its willowy branches gently blowing in the breeze, feeling its roots reaching down into the earth, and feeling the support of your own roots.

The morning sun has risen and before you, arising majestically in the golden light of a glorious dawn, is a mountain bathed in the warm sunlight of a new day, reaching almost up to the clouds. And as you glance heavenward toward its summit, you find your attention floating upward, slowly, steadily, floating upward toward its peaks. You can see, as though looking through a telescope, all the way to the top. And zooming in toward the summit you begin to see something quite familiar coming into focus. *Your vision.* The outcome you are committed to bringing about. Zoom in and let yourself **4:00** see it now. Make it real. See the world you want to create waiting for you there.

(pause)

And letting your awareness return to where you're resting near the crystal spring, you take a sip of its fresh, cool, empowering waters. Feel your sense of purpose and commitment. As you gaze again upward toward the summit, you feel a strong physical attraction toward it. A powerful motivation to reach for it. And now you can see **5:00** leading from your special place, a pathway that leads in a twisting, meandering way up the mountain to the vision you seek. With your eye you can trace the course of that path up the mountain, and see that there are a number of challenges you must face. A number of milestones you must pass, but you feel ready, willing and able.

And in your mind's eye you can picture yourself rising and starting up that path boldly, confidently. Yet as soon as you begin you see signs posted along the way.

Caution

Unexplored territory

No services along this road

6:00 You read them, but you do not heed them. You have made your decision and you are confident. You give yourself an inner signal, a cue. You feel a little invisible smile behind your upper lip, and you continue your progress, feeling your courage increasing with each step.

As you continue going higher and higher, you meet other challenges and distractions.

• A feast of food befitting a king is laid out, tempting you to stop and eat your fill, and sleep awhile. But you continue on. And as you walk you hold your head high, a signal to yourself that you are on course. You will not be stopped. You step forward with confidence.

• Not far away is the river of forgetfulness, which makes you sleepy and entices you to take refuge in oblivion, but you feel the strength to say no and you continue on.

7:00 • A beautiful garden of seductive and sensual power beckons you to give up your quest and surrender to physical pleasure, but you are committed. And you continue on, higher and higher, taking strength and satisfaction from each milestone as you pass it. From each challenge as you master it.

And now you're reaching the summit and receiving the rich reward that awaits you there. You have achieved your vision, and as you stand on top of this mountain you look back, knowing you did it. That you CAN have what you want.

And now, with your vision securely in heart, mind and body, you step off on a fluffy white cloud and rise **8:00** slowly upward.

(pause)

You are not afraid, not even surprised as you leave the planet's canopy and drift into the silent peacefulness of space. You are comfortable, peaceful and alone with your deepest thoughts and dreams as you gaze at your lovely world—a living aqueous pearl suspended in a sea of black.

And then, zooming in on various points on the planet, observing the many levels of life, hold in mind the type of planet you would like to live upon. Do you see it green and healthy? Can you see the people living upon it in harmony? Can you envision your community and **9:00** workplace as a healthy, happy place to be? Can you see yourself as part of a warm, loving family? Create your own personal vision, and feel the strong desire within to see it become reality.

(pause)

Now ask, "What is *my* special contribution? How can I use *my* special gifts to make the world a better place in which to live, whether in a small way or a large way? Whether my reward will be material or friendship, or simply the deep satisfaction that comes from working **10:00** with others to realize our fondest dreams. How can I use my special talents?" Imagine yourself committing your energy, your skill and your love to this most sacred of tasks . . . *now*.

(pause)

(A Global Vision)

Now think of yourself as one little point on the great surface of the great sphere that's travelling through space, going around and around the sun. At other points of the sphere there are other human beings, each one uniquely himself or herself, each one uniquely living his or her own life. Know that each of these individuals really wants the same thing—a safe, healthy, loving world in which to live. One that's green and productive, inhabited by happy

11:00 people. And imagine that right now, at this point in time . . . we as human beings, after looking at the history of our race . . . after seeing the useless wars and destruction, loss and pain . . . imagine that we, the people of the Earth, now have the ability to choose to achieve everyone's deepest inner wish. That we, individually,

---

Guided Visualization

To bring greater meaning to our lives we can plant deeply and firmly into our belief system not only a personal vision—the outcome that each of us is committed to see in our own life—but also a global vision, the outcome we would wish for our planet. Meditative visualization can not only take readers on a pleasant journey of the mind, but it can help us overcome our imbalances and heal our lives.

Sometime at your convenience, on a cassette tape, record five minutes of your favorite gentle music or natural sounds such as birds singing or a bubbling brook or ocean waves pounding the shore, to help your mind relax. Then, with the music or sounds continuing in the background, read Chapter 2 in a slow, calm voice. The entire reading should take about 25 or 26 minutes plus 5 minutes of introductory music. Then set aside a quiet time several times each week to relax and listen to your tape. As you listen time and again, your visions and dreams may become very clear, if they are not already.

To make a tape recording and use it for guided imagery or deep relaxation, first read the chapter through once or twice to get familiar with it. Then, at a convenient time, read it with feeling and vocal variety into a tape recorder, pausing in the appropriate places. Read it slowly onto tape. Recommended elapsed times are printed in the left margin. A "pause" lasts 10-15 seconds. The "long pause" lasts about 30 seconds. (Don't read onto tape any of the material that's in parentheses.)

If you don't like the sound of your recorded voice, you can try a couple of things: In the short term you could have someone else narrate the script on tape; in the long run you may wish to read the book *Change Your Voice, Change Your Life* by Dr. Morton Cooper. It offers suggestions about making your voice as appealing and natural as possible.

—MHM

and as a group, are now ready to choose to create the world we really want.

And by expanding your imagination a little more, become aware of the values we share, and the connection you have with everyone around you, in your family, in your community, or in the organization where you work. Know that there is a shared heritage, a shared set of values, and a shared consciousness that unites us to the **12:00** vast family of 5 billion human beings living in the fragile biosphere of this tiny planet. And through this nervous system of consciousness we all share, you can reach out and touch someone of another color, in another land, and sense the rhythm of their lives. Their challenges, their daily work. Their beauty. You can experience their joys. And feel the inner power that leads human beings to seek meaning and communion with a higher wisdom. Sensing how in our global community we all share the same resources, the same fate and the same universal human experiences and connections with those we love.

Be aware that there is a healing that our families, our communities, our organizations, our nations and our **13:00** planet must undergo in order to survive. Just as all cells of the body must become aware of disease and then share and focus their energy to heal an injured part, we must allow ourselves to see the hunger and poverty, the homelessness and suffering, to know that only through awareness, faith and right action can the community of humankind bring an end to this misery.

We are calm and receptive as we listen to that ancient voice that teaches survival of the wisest. That we can cooperate and survive. That we can eliminate this gray cancer that even now crosses our own borders turning our once exciting cities and towns into ugly, smog-choked jungles of locked doors, and the homeless, the jobless. . . . **14:00** The spreading global sickness as our oceans are poisoned by chemical wastes and the rain forests are stripped out from under us. The basis of life on our planet being weakened . . . dying. . . . That if we choose, we can reverse the gradual destruction of our air, our water, our land and our people.

Let yourself become aware of your vision for the future. Imagine yourself being carried forward through time. You can see your life developing according to your true nature and purpose. What kind of world can you see yourself growing in?

(pause)

15:00   What's the highest level of evolution for this planet that you can think of? Project ahead. Perhaps three years, or five years or ten years. Or perhaps forward to the year 2000. What is the most peaceful, the most loving, happiest, richest, most rewarding Earth you can envision?

What kind of people do you see living on this Earth? How green can you see the trees? How colorful the flowers? What kind of faces do you see around you? Follow these images. Let the energy of love within you guide you toward a clearer and clearer image of the most perfect future you can bring to mind. Become aware again of your own true nature. Feel closeness and love for those near to you. See how you fit into this new world you are creating.

16:00

(pause)

Now, feeling strength and commitment growing inside you, descend to your special place. Stepping off your comfortable white cloud, relax, feeling the gentle breeze, the bright colors sparkling in the sun, the swirling pool of crystal water.

Now let yourself become consciously aware of your major goals, the steps that lead to your vision. Your outcome.

Specifically, what are the major challenges you will meet?

17:00   (pause)

What are the hurdles you must cross?
And what are the milestones?

(pause)

How, specifically, will you know when you have dealt successfully with each of these challenges?

Become aware of them now. And one by one picture yourself achieving your goals. Feel yourself accomplishing the first task. Feel the victory as you achieve it with ease and grace.

(pause)

Moving steadily onto the next goal, once again experience yourself winning. Really experience physically, emotionally and spiritually, each accomplishment all the way to and including your vision, the final outcome you

18:00 want to produce.

(long pause)

Picture yourself achieving your vision. Feel how good it feels. The joy. The fulfillment. The satisfaction. You've arrived. You've succeeded. You are feeling all the feelings you knew you'd feel. And as you feel the love and the

19:00 peace that come with this achievement, return once again to the sound of the spring. Into your special place.

Within you, feel the feelings of commitment and dedication to your vision more strongly than ever.

With your feet firmly on the ground you are now certain in your heart that with each step you are drawing closer and closer to your vision. You sense the energy rising through your being. Power fills your limbs. Your garden, in its beauty, and all the life around you energize you. You begin to run. Slowly at first. And then with more and more energy as you stride effortlessly into the forest. You run faster and faster, and you notice you are in company with the animals of the forest. A deer leaps in

20:00 joy alongside you. An eagle soars above, calling out encouragement to you. And as you gather speed, you know at the deepest level . . . you know where you are going.

And you WILL succeed. You realize that there will be situations, people, secondary goals and emotional challenges that will threaten to distract, divert and discourage you. To hypnotize and seduce you from your purpose. To intimidate and frighten you. But you know you'll ignore these temptations. You will stand firm and advance confidently and enthusiastically toward your chosen goal. You're clearly focused and in touch with your will power and your strength. You are saying yes to your vision. Feel that feeling energize you, and breathe

21:00 deeply into it. Breathe it throughout all the cells of your body.

And now, become aware again of the very next step— the next objective along your path. Deep within, you know you are ready and willing to take this next step forward, to continue to ascend the path, and feeling the powerful attraction of your vision, you have the courage to go for it. You can do it. Nothing and no one is worth stopping for as long as you are attuned with those you

22:00 love. You have the tools to deal with any obstacles along the way.

You know now that you can overcome anything. Feel the enthusiasm, the energy within, growing stronger.

And remember, today's world needs you to be the best you can be. Whatever you can do, or dream you can, begin it ... and doors will open for you. Boldness has genius, power and magic in it.

The owner of this book is welcome to make a copy of this chapter on tape for personal use.

Chapter Three:
Crisis as a Turning Point: What Sickness Taught Me About Healing

by Mark Macy

His background. Writer and editor of numerous computer and telecommunications manuals and three nonfiction books on systems solutions—*Last Chance for Peace* (pseud. 1985), *Solutions for a Troubled World* (ed. 1987) and the current anthology. Subscriber to numerous worldview organizations and publications: World Future Society, IFDA, Institute of Noetic Sciences, WorldWatch, *New Options Newsletter*, *World Press Review*, Global Education Associates. Innate skills include musical ear, creative thinking, language aptitude. Cultivated skills include communication, systems thinking, problem solving, intuitiveness.

His chapter. A bout with cancer taught the author that curing one's illness is not the same as healing one's life. The first technique sweeps away current symptoms and perhaps explores some of their causes, while the second brings greater balance and vitality to one's body, mind and spirit. Healing our lives can bring benefits to ourselves, our societies and our world that are wonderful almost beyond description.

> *Until we can acknowledge our heart as our link to the spirit world, there is no chance of healing our lives, nor of healing our world.*

Crisis as a Turning Point:
What Sickness Taught Me About Healing

by Mark Macy

When a person gets cancer, s/he soon learns that a *major* change will have to be made if a long, happy life is desirable. A life once centered around greasy meals, caffeine and perhaps alcohol may become a life rich in grains, fresh fruits and vegetables. A life of repressed feelings, resentment and mistrust may become a life of openness, love and trust. Essentially, life is turned upside down. It takes a bit of time for the digestive system, the organs and the ten trillion cells in the body to get used to the changes, but gradually one is rewarded with a better life, greater happiness, and a more integrated system.

When overgrown cultures that have enjoyed using natural resources to their fullest according to the economic ideas of Karl Marx and Adam Smith ravage and poison their environments beyond their ancestors' wildest nightmares and trigger an upheaval of the global climate, they soon learn that *major* changes are in order. That learning process is underway today as perestroika and glasnost become the new battle cry of Eastern Europe, and as recycling, moderation, ecoawareness, and community-building become the latest passions in the West.

I have been preoccupied for nearly twenty years by world crises, but it is only in the past two years that I've become thoroughly immersed in crisis and healing of a personal nature. After cancer surgery in July 1988 I gave a copy of my book *Solutions for a Troubled World* to the surgeon, John Day (who is also a yogi and since the operation has become a friend of mine). Glancing through the book he commented, "Mark, I think you'd better heal yourself before you try to heal the world." Advice well taken. This book, which was well underway as a sequel to *Solutions*, was moved to the back burner to simmer as I set off to heal my life. Gradually I began interweaving the planetary visions of the book's authors with my new-found insights into personal healing, and the book very slowly started to take an interesting shape. Some authors dropped out of the project, feeling the book was becoming too much of a personal thing (you see, in two years' time I had transformed from a head person to a heart person, as though Star Trek's Mr. Spock had suddenly become Dr. McCoy, and my writing began to reflect a confusion of ideas and feelings. For the first time in my life I became absorbed in my own needs!) Gradually my life became more balanced . . . and then so did the book. New authors joined the project as the book was rearranged, personal material being rounded up and channelled into this chapter. Since the book took shape in parallel with my new life, its development and completion have brought tremendous mood swings, satisfaction and knowledge.

Of the myriad facts and figures I've gathered over the past three years, one truth stands above the rest: When we look at crisis as a catastrophe it only darkens our disposition and makes matters worse, but when we accept it as a turning point it can give us, quite literally, new life. Accepting crisis as an opportunity gives us the inspiration and determination we need to embark on a healthy new way of living.

This is as true for the world as it is for me. I wouldn't go so far as to say that the brown clouds above our cities all have silver linings, but I would certainly say that the time is ripe for healing the planet, and to get the job done we can use the oceans of information now pouring in from all points on the globe, not just on subjects of world affairs but also on healing in general. Life is, after all, interconnected at all levels. What applies to us individually can often be projected outward to apply equally well to families, organizations, communities, nations, and the world at large.

We all need to pave our own customized paths to personal healing, as no two people are alike. Even so, all paths lead back to certain basic truths shared by all of us, such as:

- Unconditional love can make our heart healthy.
- Exercise and wholesome nutrition can help keep a body fit.
- Appropriate education, sights and sounds can nurture a wholesome mind.

• Meditation, relaxation, guided imagery, and Qi Gong (Eisenberg) can keep our life in balance.

• Knowing ourself and maintaining intimate ties with our divine essence can bring profound peace of mind.

So exercise, good eating habits, love, right education, relaxation, self-realization and spirituality are among the basic standards of personal health, but beyond such basics we each need to determine for ourself what keeps us healthy and happy.

Likewise, each country, community and group needs to build its own path toward social and planetary healing above a stable foundation of global standards and values—things that we know with fair certainty to be vital for healthy groups and a healthy planet in the future. These include:

• cleaning up the environment (reversing acid rain, water and air pollution, destruction of the ozone layer, radiation fallout, destruction of rain forests), equity in world trade, ending wars, resolving conflicts, eliminating the arms race among nations, conserving resources, ensuring plenty of food is distributed to everyone, eliminating terrorism and international drug trafficking, and protecting the rights of women and minorities (Macy)

• global education (Muller)

• providing families what they need for stability and love, including jobs, health care, child care, elder care, family leave, services for elderly, shelter, and safe neighborhoods and cities (Clabes)

• changing our focus from economic growth to character development (Wachtel, Rahnema)

• gratifying children's needs for love, creativity, communication skills and discipline (Schaeffer)

• rebuilding or replacing economics to better account for today's complexities (Henderson, Pietila)

• spreading the skills of citizen diplomacy to everyone interested in being immersed in other cultures (McDonald)

• ensuring healthy, stable populations (Liang/Wang).

To heal the planet it is time to come to a planetary consensus on what is fundamentally wholesome for the world and its five billion inhabitants, and to carve a simple but thorough framework of global standards and values that can act as an anchor for all social systems in the stormy seas ahead.

The world is undergoing enormous change, and solving the problems we face today will require still more change. Global healing will require further integration of diverse nations, cultures and religions. That will mean changes for everyone—a careful move out of our comfort zones. And that, of course, means stress. Stress is unavoidable in most modern societies, but it can be overcome with an attitude of curiosity and involvement, a sense that we are not mere puppets, and a view of change as a stimulating opportunity (Borysenko) rather than a threat. That will be useful to remember as increased globalization in the coming years brings not only the benefits of growing compatibility but also the rigors of stress.

When chronic stress and its accompanying despair are ignored or accepted as normal, our body starts to receive a "die" message from our mind (Siegel), our immune system weakens, and we develop colds, cancer and other diseases. It is vital that we all learn to deal with stress. Stay curious, get involved, take control of our life, and enjoy the unexpected opportunities that come our way . . . even if they are cleverly disguised as tragedies.

Animals removed from their familiar social environments, caged, and subjected to experiments in a cold, sterile laboratory suffer chronic stress which causes the presence of hormones (adrenaline and cortisol) in the body which in turn suppress the immune system. (Borysenko)

With a weakened immune system animals become far more prone to cancer and other diseases. (Siegel)

So, animals removed from their comfortable, natural environments are more prone to getting sick.

What is a natural environment for people today? Our social surroundings have changed a lot over time—from nomadic tribes to small communities to large societies (Schaeffer)—making that question difficult to answer. Yet regardless of the massive changes in society, the family has remained the most basic and stable natural setting for us down through the ages. (Clabes) Furthermore, a situation in which individuals and their families are entwined in a sense of community and trust with others (through church or neighborhood or whatever) seems to be a prerequisite of well-being. (Rahnema)

From this I would conclude that only if we fit into a loving family in a trusting community can we enjoy the best health our body-mind can achieve. Sadly, that is not always the case. There are many homes where love is an exception and either abuse or neglect is the rule. (Clabes) It would be nice if the workplace as well as the home were built on love and trust since we spend so much time there, but unfortunately that is even less often the case.

So when it comes to healing our societies it is in the families and the communities where we must begin. And if we continue to spend a big share of our life at work, we'd better transform the workplace into a place of love and trust.

Love

Love makes the world go 'round. That may not make much head sense to a physicist though it makes a great deal of heart sense to anyone on the road to genuine healing and happiness. To find peace and good health for our world today we must open our hearts to it.

The subject of love is new to my writing—a silver lining in the dark cloud of cancer. After my illness, my heart openly embraced the *feeling* of love, but my head seemed to require some sort of reason or explanation before accepting the *concept*. So for my brain's sake I assembled an acceptable definition of love from two sources: 1) a message I received during an encounter with Gurumayi Chidvilasananda, a lovely, glowing goddess of the international Siddha Yoga organization when she visited Denver in 1989 and enveloped a ballroom-full of people in her life-changing *shakti* force (this young woman has one foot on earth, the other in the spirit world), and 2) the audiotape *The Road Less Travelled: Love*. (Peck)

As youngsters we build around us a wall of ego or "selfness" to protect ourself from the emotional bumps and jabs of society. It becomes a case of "me against the rest of the world." Later in life, not only do we hold onto that emotional shell, but we project it into our social systems, so that our life as an adult becomes a clumsy compromise between protecting our self from the rest of society and protecting our society from the rest of the world.

The way to find love, trust and happiness is not to obliterate our shell of ego (which is, literally, "self" destruction), but to extend our ego to include other people, things and groups around us. To pull them into our self and make them part of us. As we get more adept at love and feel its tremendous benefits, we can broaden our ego to absorb more and more of the world around us. Love, in short, is the result of accepting people and things into our ego.

As we broaden our ego around a growing realm of the universe, we gain an intimate knowledge of the people and things we've encompassed. Not necessarily the type of knowledge we get from reading a book or tracing a family tree (though it could include knowledge of that type), but more an intuitive understanding. This is something that an orthodox scientist and others here in the West may not acknowledge in principle though they live it in private. Most of us feel it every day of our lives among family and close friends.

For long-term pleasure and security, love must be bolstered by commitment to loved ones—the people and groups we've allowed into our ego boundaries—and on-going efforts to satisfy their needs while preserving our individuality and making sure our own needs are met. Through these efforts we gain a deeper and deeper understanding of the people and things we love.

In Eastern thought there can eventually come a mystical union between self and the universe, a state of pure love and bliss called *nirvana*. It brings an intuitive awareness of life in its entirety. It is believed that the tiny portion of the universe we experience through our senses is just that: a tiny portion of reality, an illusion. To be fully a part of life is to become one with the universe. To do so we must overcome the notion that we are one thing, and God or Nature or the world is another thing; we are all one. Instead of saying, "I love God," or "I love Nature," or I respect "Allah," which imply that we are *apart from* the divine essence, we would say "I *am* God" or "I *am* Nature" or "I *am* Shiva" or "I *am* Yahweh" or "I *am* Allah," to acknowledge that the infinite power is *a part of* us. Then we start moving in that direction.

We can get a brief taste or glimpse of love when we "fall head over heels" into a romantic love encounter. Our ego boundaries collapse as we merge with the other person. Similarly, we can get a taste of nirvana with sex or drugs as, again, the ego collapses. But alas, the glow soon wears off, the ego is quickly put back into place, and any sense of security derived from these shallow experiences is false and short-lived.

Fostering a life of unconditional love of self, family, friends and world is not an easy process for many people, especially men who have had to close their heart and hide their feelings to protect themselves while growing up. Nonetheless, to heal one's life requires a sense of love underlying one's day-to-day, year-to-year life. How one finds it is not so important; finding it is crucial to healing our life. Joining spiritual groups can help—the international Siddha Yoga organization, the Swadhyaya movement in India (Rahnema), or open-hearted Christian, Moslem, Buddhist or Jewish groups worldwide.

Personal meditation is a vital skill. I've had immense pleasure playing with my new-found feelings. Sometimes in meditation I like to imagine a ball of energy surrounding my heart. To feel love for a special person or place or thing, I imagine the energy bulging outward and absorbing that subject of my warmth. The ball can grow to any shape and size imaginable. I can absorb the entire world in my love. On a good meditation day my body bristles as I perform this spiritual exercise. Or, sometimes in meditation I imagine my brain moving slowly down my spine as though in an elevator until my awareness is in my heart rather than my head. My breathing automatically deepens and I can regard my world and myself from a perspective of pure love rather than logic, feelings rather than ideas. There is a complete immersion in love, inspiration and pleasant images that is almost beyond description. Another way to get there in meditation is to envision your brain as a boat on a gentle, nourishing sea. Drop anchor to the heart and pull the boat slowly downward through the nourishing fluid, into the heart . . . and *bing*, life is light.

These are more than just mental games or tricks; they are among the many methods of igniting the God potential in us. This God potential (or Qi or chee or shakti or kundalini or Holy Spirit) is the life force within us that can bring us profound love, peace, happiness and good health (Rahnema). Many people when told they have God potential in them, tend to react, "If it's in me then why can't I see it or feel it?" The answer: just as there is butter in fresh milk that can't be seen until it is churned, the God within us can't be perceived or used until it is properly processed. (Hayes) Or, just as the gasoline in crude oil is invisible and useless before the refining process, the pure love of our divine essence cannot be used until it has been refined. This refinement of spirit is achieved through various forms of meditation.

Whether finding genuine love with another person or moving further along the road toward nirvana, it helps to acknowledge our heart as a center of intuition and feelings, not just a blood pump. Our heart is the link to the spirit world. Until most of us can acknowledge and feel that, I believe there is no chance of healing our lives, nor of healing our planet. Using rational plans and "head" solutions to achieve isolated targets or to address individual crises—cleaning up toxic wastes, disarming the nuclear arsenals, restoring the rain forests, turning the deserts green, ending hunger—can only have limited results. Only when we get to the very heart of the matter can we find a holistic solution. If we can broaden our ego to absorb our family, family troubles will soon be resolved. If we all love our world, the planet's problems will soon be resolved.

Wholesome Body-Mind Nourishment

After building a life upon love, probably the next most important step toward my healing was getting into the habit of taking into the system only things that will help it. After cancer, that subject became a top preoccupation for two years, and after a lot of researching and reading I found four apparent kernels of truth about human nourishment:

1. Food, air and information. Right nourishment applies to everything we take into our body—not just food but also the air we breathe into our lungs, minerals and molecules absorbed through the skin as during warm baths and showers, and the knowledge and information we allow into our minds.

Knowledge is taken into the mind mostly through the eyes and ears in the form of energy, whether as sound waves from a teacher's voice or tape recorder, or as light bouncing off a printed page or emitted from a TV set or computer screen. Energy is encoded in such a way that it is meaningful to the brain. Certain sounds, certain images, certain letters, certain words hold meaning for us. The brain accepts the information we see and hear, and shapes our attitudes and behavior accordingly.

For the system to thrive, the food, air and coded energy taken in must be pure and wholesome. Impurities in these will cause problems in the structure and behavior of the system. As one of this book's authors has written elsewhere:

> During more than 20 years of commuting between my little village in the Hudson Valley and Manhattan (where I worked at the UN), nobody ever saw me read a newspaper. As a result, I was immune to New York's and to the world's daily neuroses, and hence an infinitely happier person. I would read, every morning on the train, writings of some of the great masters of literature and philosophy, to brace myself against the mental beating that awaited me in the gigantic city. Again, in the evening, my old masters lifted me to higher spirits and helped me to face my family as a good-natured, normal human being.
>
> I am as particular about the nutrition of my mind as I am with the nourishment of my body. I seek the food, news, images, words and sounds that I consider good for myself—that is, that bring me health, happiness, and self-fulfillment—and I carefully avoid toxic materials that others wish to impose on me.
>
> Perhaps someday the news media will change and bring happiness and hope to the people. (Muller)

2. Food allergies. Everyone has a unique set of substances that are harmful to them, substances that are generally harmless or even beneficial and nutritious to other people. A person suffers an allergic reaction whenever one of these substances is brought into the body, whether through the mouth, or through the nose while breathing, or through the skin as during a skin-type allergy test. The reactions can range from indigestion and dry skin to sinus congestion and chills, from anxiety and depression to schizophrenia and chronic insomnia. (Forman)

Some allergies are congenital and stay with us throughout life while others change as our eating habits change or as we move to a different region where the air is different for breathing, where drinking water and foods are different. We commonly develop one of these temporary allergies by eating the same food too often. It can become a vicious circle (Wachtel) in which the body develops a love-hate relationship with a food. It craves more and more of the food that it cannot properly digest, and toxins build up in the body. The symptoms of allergy are often regarded by allergists as allergic/addictive reactions. As a rule of thumb, if there's a food that we truly crave and truly love, and which we eat almost every day, we are probably allergic to it.

3. Mixing and matching foods. Not only is it important what foods we eat, but also in what combinations we eat them (Diamond). The following *Fit for Life* rules helped get my digestive tract quickly into shape and stay in shape after my bout with colon cancer and the ensuing surgery:

• Fruits are the easiest foods to digest. They pass through the stomach in 15 to 30 minutes. Eaten daily, they can do an excellent job of keeping the body cleaned out. But, they are valuable only when eaten on an empty stomach. If eaten with cooked starch or protein, fruit stays in the stomach as long as the other foods and loses most of its cleansing qualities. So as a foundation for clean living, for the first several hours after I awaken, I eat nothing but fresh fruit.

• Vegetables. Lots of fresh or lightly steamed, nonstarchy vegetables are a healthy addition to all meals and between-meal snacks, from lunch until bedtime.

• Protein or starch. Eat vegetables either with protein foods like meat and cheese, or with starchy foods like bread, cooked potatoes and grains, but avoid mixing protein and starch. At first, this may be difficult to accept, since the culinary traditions throughout most of the world are based on this mix—meat and potatoes, rice and fish, arroz con pollo, spaghetti and meat sauce, sandwiches, cereal and milk, potatoes au gratin, fish and chips.

Protein is digested by acid in the stomach. Starch is digested by alkaline fluids in the mouth. Eaten together, they can putrefy in the stomach and intestine, the body's 98-degree pressure cooking system, as the acid and alkaline juices neutralize each other and form salt water. A traditional feast containing overcooked meats, cheeses, fats, breads, potatoes and grains can rot in the body for three days or longer, causing large amounts of toxins to be absorbed into the tissues. Toxic buildup weakens the system and leads to a wide range of diseases, one of the most talked about being cancer.

In a nutshell, then, I eat nothing but fruit for the first several hours after I awaken, then some whole-grain snacks. For main meals I enjoy fresh vegetables with starchy foods (breads, grains, potatoes . . .) or a little protein (nuts, meat, cheese), but I usually avoid mixing protein with starch. I like to eat meat now and then, but I eat it lean and rare. Fat is hard to digest, and overcooked meat is essentially a mild poison with little nutritional value. (Diamond)

4. More plants, less meat. And finally, recent studies show that fruits and vegetables, not meats, are the healthiest foods for the human body. In China, many families have lived in the same provinces for many generations, eating the same foods today that their ancestors ate a century ago. Diets may vary widely from province to province throughout China, but through the years each province has preserved most of its culinary traditions. That provides an ideal setting to test just how healthy or unhealthy various eating habits are when carried on year after year, generation after generation.

Such a study was undertaken jointly by the Chinese Academy of Medical Science, the Chinese Academy of Preventive Medicine, Cornell University (US), and Oxford University (UK). Their results, published in September 1989, provide the most conclusive look ever taken at just what constitutes healthy eating habits. The daily intake of the average person in the healthiest provinces in China comprises a pound of rice, a half-pound of vegetables (spinach, cabbage, carrots, mushrooms, water chestnuts, snow peas, sprouts, etc.), a quarter-pound of starchy root vegetables, and just over one ounce of meat.

Interpreting this diet to apply more generally to developed countries, the first step is to make sure the foods we buy are free of preservatives, hormones, pesticides and other chemicals, a common problem with processed foods, meats, eggs, peanuts and grains (studies have found that many of the pesticides sprayed onto wheat fields are still on the wheat when processed into bread and placed on the market shelf).

The next step in adapting the Chinese data to Western life styles is to get into a mindset that meals should be high in whole grain products of rice, wheat, oats, corn, etc. (about a pound or pound and a half a day, on the average); also high in fresh or frozen mixed vegetables (say, a half-pound); with very little meat.

To summarize nourishment, then, I have become aware of what I take into my system and how it affects me. I need to consciously avoid toxins until it becomes a habit to do so. These include substances that are toxic to everyone, such as animal fat, alcohol and harmful alkaloids (the notorious "ine-s" which range from the fairly mild caffeine and nicotine to the more powerful heroine, morphine, codeine and cocaine). The toxins also include my own personal allergens—milk, eggs and wheat, the three principal foods of my childhood. They include violence and promiscuity in the media which I read and watch. And they include mistrust, deception and resentment that I used to allow into my being during my dealings with others. I have come to welcome clean water and air, fresh fruits and vegetables, trust and love, and fiction and nonfiction books, articles, TV programs and movies that deal with real human situations without pandering to my basic human weaknesses. In short, I welcome into my system the things that keep my life wholesome.

At the national and planetary levels that fundamental principle needs to become the core of economics: We must welcome into our social systems only resources that keep them wholesome. Phase out petroleum, plutonium and other social allergens and poisons as we learn to live lightly on the earth. Or perhaps economics is beyond salvage, and a new means of inhabiting the planet is needed. (Henderson, Pietila) In any case, I believe that a sustainable ratio between resources and system needs must be the basis for any science that does for social systems what the field of nutrition does for the body.

Wholesome Behavior

To heal from my sickness has required several basic changes in my values and attitudes. I had a basic mistrust of people, and not just strangers. I even questioned whether friends and loved ones had my best interests in mind. I used to be competitive and driven to win at everything. I was a "type-A" personality, fast with my thinking, eating, and driving, endlessly impatient. I used to do as little planning as possible, just keeping in mind a fairly clear picture of the final goal and a general idea of the work involved. I would let inspiration, creativity and impulse fill in the steps. As a result I would find myself busy at my desk at odd hours of the day and night. Many of the results were inspired and creative, but the disorganized, unplanned behavior eventually took its toll in the form of stress and a weakened immune system.

So with the preparation of this book I'm setting a new course for my life. I'm finding a deep trust of humanity, of myself, and especially of loved ones close to me. I've been toning down my obsessions to compete, succeed, and achieve huge, perhaps unrealistic goals. I'm slowing down, enjoying more the food I eat and the scenery I'm driving through. I'm learning how to go about calmly changing things that bother me and accepting what cannot be changed. I've had to better organize my life, breaking down the jobs ahead of me into small, clearly defined steps. I lay the steps out on a calendar.

For world peace, all nations will need to undergo a similar adjustment to some of their basic values and attitudes. The economic ideas by which nations interact in today's world need to be rebuilt upon greater trust and cooperation, less aggressive competition. The industrialized countries need to temper their drive and obsession to grow-grow-grow and produce-produce-produce to the detriment of society and environment. (Henderson, Pietila)

We will need long-term planning, with world development goals broken down into small, clearly defined steps which will bring struggling countries up to healthy standards. What's likely to emerge in the coming years is a global value system which nations, religions, communities and other social systems will feel comfortable incorporating into their own value systems to provide an underlying sense of compatibility and security within and among groups all around the world.

A couple of months after surgery I began to see a psychologist, Richard Shane, who my surgeon suggested might be able to help me unravel deep-seated imbalances and issues that I didn't even know I had. As is common among cancer patients (if not among most everyone), my chronic emotional imbalances for many years of adulthood seemed normal to me. I thought life was supposed to be like that.

We tried guided imagery, hypnosis and a peculiar process called breathwork in which I would lie on the floor on pillows, knees up in the air, breathing as quickly and deeply as I could for 45 minutes. Richard told me to feel free to yell or cry or laugh, whatever I felt like doing but, frankly, I just felt silly. After these sessions my hands would be tingly and my body would feel cleansed from all the oxygenated blood flowing through it. A nice glowing feeling on those cold winter nights, but no miracles.

Richard also tried to get me to move my consciousness from my head to various other parts of the body. I had little success doing that at the time. He would encourage me to feel and describe any uncomfortable sensations anywhere inside me. I'd never been able to feel things like this, nor even tried or thought about feeling my feelings. During one session I had a vague feeling that a tightness might be in my stomach area. He told me to move my consciousness to my stomach. I tried my best to comply, but in the back of my mind was a persistent thought: This is *very* unusual. Within a year I phased out of therapy. I continued playing with my consciousness in private meditation, finding profound peace when I learned to bring it to the heart area. I didn't realize at the time that the work with Richard had planted a healing seed deep within me.

Two years after the operation a disturbing cycle emerged. A week or two of deep, restful sleep, utter bliss and love of life would be followed by another week of fitful sleep, uneasiness, tightness of stomach, dissatisfaction with my life and job, and an urge to leave home for a week or two or a month to seclude myself in a forest cabin near an ocean. It started out as a subtle cycle, but eventually became quite extreme. The pleasant up-cycles grew shorter while the down-cycles grew longer. It was like a splinter festering beneath the skin—working itself upward, then receding; rising higher, and receding . . . gradually, painfully moving toward the surface. Some days I became a bit nauseous, other days I'd have pain in the lower back. One day I found some crimson blood after going to the bathroom—a danger signal— and I grew concerned that my cancer might be rallying for a second attack. I started making appointments the next day for medical tests.

That Saturday night (August 18, 1990) during one of my sleepless periods, while resting on the couch I moved my attention to my heart, then focused it even lower to the abdomen where Qi Gong masters focus theirs. I went into very deep, heavy breathing, and my body went into a curled-up, yoga-like position. Waves of fear, anger and resentment surged through me and I cried a bit. When it ended an hour later I was sweaty and exhausted, felt remarkably cleansed, and fell into a deep sleep.

The next day I told Regina about the experience. It reminded her of a "rebirthing" procedure she had been led through some years earlier. I told her that I felt my experience would probably be a breakthrough for me and for the family. She said she thought the family was doing pretty well as it was. On the surface, yes, I replied, but lately, during my down-cycles I had been feeling as though I could explode at any moment. I had been yelling at Aaron occasionally for no good reason, throwing angry comments and glances at Regina when I felt irritated by one thing or another, being often unaccepting of my mother-in-law who lives with us.

I awoke Sunday feeling as though I were glowing. The family seemed to be glowing as well. It was a wonderful day, but Sunday night, again, I got little sleep. After dragging through work Monday I piled into the car with Regina and Aaron and we went to our weekly session with our network chiropractor, Rick Kronen, and the most amazing thing happened. As I lay on my back on the table, I gave in to an incredible urge to start breathing quickly and deeply. I began to perspire profusely as my body started undulating in a sort of yogic exercise. My first two fingers of each hand became glued to the thumbs, and I was unable to open my hands, which became clenched tightly to my chest. My jaw froze, locking my mouth in a small o, and I was unable to speak. This continued nearly an hour, followed by a 15 minute crying jag. Finally I emerged with strained muscles, drenched shirt and a glowing feeling.

Regina witnessed the ordeal and grew a bit concerned, but Rick assured us that "the wave," as he calls it, is a fairly common occurrence among his patients. He himself has gone through it a half dozen times.

Monday night, energized by "the wave," I stayed up all night to finish this chapter and wrap up the book. It's now very early Tuesday morning. If any more of these surprises spring up in the coming weeks hoping to be published, they'll have to wait for the next book, for right now I feel that I've turned the corner and am well on the road to healing my life. I'll proceed with the medical tests I've scheduled, but I already know what the results will be. My festering emotional sores have been opened up to the fresh air, and I'm in a healing mode.

A Well-Integrated Structure

Rewiring the system for greater stresses. Rick (the network chiropractor) compares the system of nerves in a stressed individual to the electrical wiring in a rickety old house. Our spinal cord passes through the vertebrae in the backbone like a length of string passed through donuts stacked one on top of the other. With the emotional bumps and bruises of life, the bones misalign, the nerves become crimped or strained, and we develop an abnormal sense of reality. As blockages develop, the body weakens, and it can handle less and less stress. Through network chiropractic, Rick clears out the blockages to allow the unrestrained flow of chi or life force throughout the body. Once cleared, we can handle stress very well. I certainly hope that's true, since we live in very stressful times.

As usual, I had my doubts about the effectiveness of the process but kept them to myself during the first four months of visits. It was the incredible experience yesterday (August 20) which made a believer of me. The more I experience of healing, the less skeptical I become of the procedures at the fringes of science and medicine, such as rewiring the body through chiropractic therapy, deep tissue massage, and rebirthing.

Many countries, especially in the Third World, are poorly wired with dilapidated networks for transportation, communication and electricity. These networks are unable to accommodate the modern machines and appliances distributed to homes and offices throughout the industrialized world. Part of the emerging global plan will be the rewiring of the Third World to accommodate the tremendous flow of people, materials and energies (albeit a sustainable flow!) that will typify social systems of the next century.

Fish in a Polluted Stream

Sometimes I feel like a fish in a polluted river. Powerless. There's not much I can do, personally, to halt the bad habits, racial and gender discrimination, cruel jokes, polluted air, and other aspects of society's tainted waters. I can only swim with the other fish . . . live with them or die with them. Before getting married I moved a lot, apparently hoping somewhere in the back of my mind that I'd be swimming upstream beyond the pollution. No such luck. Now I've resigned myself to the fact that it's everywhere, and the secret is to learn to live with it. To do what I can to improve my immediate surroundings but not to become immersed beyond the point where I can devote most of my love and energy to the essential things in my life—books, music, family and friends.

• I'll continue to enjoy an occasional serving of food that's fine tasting but poor nutritionally—the fatty, sugary, salty, deadly cuisine that makes American mouths water. If I'm eating alone or with loved ones at home, it's wholesome foods—whole grain breads and pastas, fresh vegetables and fruits, and maybe a bit of fish or poultry. But if I'm out in public at a restaurant or barbecue or potluck I'll enjoy what's available.

• I'll still laugh at a funny joke of dubious taste when I'm with a group of friends. It's healthier to laugh and keep comfortable friendships than to latch onto rigid principles and alienate myself by heaping guilt upon others. It would be nice if empathy and respect were omnipresent among races and between genders to remove the humor and appeal from such jokes—and I believe that that time is coming sooner than we think—but for now it is too big a struggle to fight the toxic, powerful currents of society.

• I no longer feel very guilty driving a car to work. Colorado gets little rainfall, which ensures a sparse population scattered across vast stretches of arid land, which in turn provides too small a tax base to support an effective mass transit system and safe bicycle paths in the existing market economy. Many people live more than 10 miles from work, as I do, so driving is the rule; busing and biking are the exceptions. The only solution is to overhaul American government (for long-term planning) and the American economy (for sustainable development) to the point where we can guarantee the construction of an entirely new transportation system. That is obviously beyond my power. So in an era of dwindling petroleum and dirty air, what's a person to do when society provides neither the incentive nor the means for each of us to make the ecologically right choice? I find it effective to go with society's existing currents and save my energy for important causes rather than to expend it trying to correct many imbalances that are beyond my control.

What's a fish to do when it realizes it lives in a polluted river?

• Move to a new river? No, I like this river. Besides, they're all polluted in one way or another nowadays.

• Purify the river? That would be the best possible solution, but obviously it's beyond my power.

• Live in today's circumstances in as happy and healthy a fashion as I possibly can? You bet! But for me, that must include cooperating with people who are getting to the root of today's problems and are working to clean up the river.

Healing an illness involves looking through the symptoms to the causes, and dealing with those.

Healing one's life always includes a transition to a sense of unconditional love of planet, society, family and self.

References

Joan Borysenko, *Minding the Body, Mending the Mind*, (Bantam Books, 1988)

Harvey and Marilyn Diamond, *Fit for Life*, (Warner Books Inc, 1985)

Judy Clabes, Chapter 4 of this book

David Eisenberg, Chapter 1 of this book

Robert Forman, *How to Control Your Allergies*, (Larchmont Books, 1979)

Peter Hayes, *The Supreme Adventure; The experience of Siddha Yoga*, (Dell Publishing, 1988)

Hazel Henderson, Chapter 9 of this book

Liang Jimin and Wang Xiangying, Chapter 5 of this book

Mark Macy (Ed.), *Solutions for a Troubled World*, (Earthview Press, 1987)

John McDonald, Chapter 11 of this book

Robert Muller, *Most of All They Taught Me Happiness* (World Happiness and Cooperation, 1989)

M. Scott Peck, *The Road Less Travelled*, (Simon and Schuster)

Hilkka Pietila, Chapter 14 of this book

Majid Rahnema, Chapter 7 of this book

Joseph Schaeffer, Chapter 8 of this book

Bernie Siegel, *Love, Medicine and Miracles*, (Harper & Row, 1988)

Paul Wachtel, Chapter 6 of this book

Chapter Four:
The Family: Back to Basics

by Judith Clabes

Her background. Editor of *The Kentucky Post* and recipient of numerous honors and first-place writing awards as a journalist and former educator. Her many published works include a syndicated weekly newspaper column, a book on women journalists (*New Guardians of the Press*), and a guide for using newspapers to teach disadvantaged children. A subject of radio, TV, print interviews and a speaker before diverse audiences. Toured Southern Africa and USSR as representative of US news organizations. Member and elected leader of many groups, including a statewide task force on runaway youths. Special interests include children and family issues. Honorary doctorate of Law.

Her chapter. The US has family problems quite different from China's (see the chapter by Liang Jimin and Wang Xiangying) but no less serious. Ms. Clabes mixes national and international statistics with parental concern to illustrate the need to restore stability in the most basic of social systems—the family. Without stability in the family, children cannot be well-adjusted and happy, and nations cannot be secure.

Family is the singlemost important means of perpetuating values, nurturing individuals, building self-esteem and providing stability.

The Family: Back to Basics

by Judith G. Clabes

The family is the only social institution present in every single society throughout history. Getting back to basics means getting down to family issues, and that is an imperative today if we hope to see a bright tomorrow.

The family as an institution is the single most important means of perpetuating values, nurturing individuals, building self-esteem and providing stability in any society. Indeed, families are the bedrock of a stable society. Our families provide for us a sense of the past, a oneness with the present and a vision of the future. It is where we have been, where we are and where we are going. Nothing is more basic than that. It is confidence, permanence, stability, security—all the things we have needed to get us through the ups and downs of life. Nothing lays for us a firmer foundation.

Certainly, each of us as individuals seeks meaningful personal relationships that give definition to our lives and depth to our sense of self. We need the kinds of familial relationships and comfortable security that prepare us to deal with the larger world in acceptable ways. This is what family is for, and it is why family is so basic to the very workings of any society. Indeed, a strong family unit is a nation's most valuable institution. It instills values and passes along a sense of responsibility and commitment to others. As individual human beings, we thrive on the caring concern of others who think we're important and special. As individuals who have had that kind of support, we are better prepared to make a positive contribution to society at large.

The US Census Bureau defines a family as a group of two or more persons related by birth, by marriage or adoption and residing together in a household. According to their latest figures, there are 62.7 million families in the US, the average size being 3.23. Almost 50 percent of these families have children under 18. Eighty percent involve a married couple and 16 percent are headed by women.

We know too, however, that great diversity has developed in basic family patterns. The traditional family fitting the profile of the popular 50s TV program, Father Knows Best, is no longer the norm. Less than 10 percent of US families fit the description of working father, stay-at-home mother and at least two children. Instead, we are developing a new definition of "traditional" family: By 1995, stepfamilies (or blended families) will outnumber the old traditional families and the Norman Rockwell family portrait will be redrawn. We make families, unmake them, remake them in ways and numbers heretofore unimagined. Yet we seek to form family bonds, whatever the configuration may be, because that is the human thing to do. Our family fabric can be woven in many ways, certainly. If we're lucky, it becomes a fine heirloom quilt, stitched over years with love and caring and nurturing and commitment and deep values that don't go away.

All of us are not lucky.

We don't need statistics to tell us that today's families are under enormous pressures—economic and social—and that too many human beings, lacking the caring support of others, are homeless, helpless, hungry, hostile, angry, misfit, misguided, mistreated, poor, illiterate, disenfranchised, drug- or alcohol-addicted, rootless, purposeless, abused or abusive.

The complexities of coping are becoming, well, a whole lot more complex.

R. Sargent Shriver, former director of the Peace Corps, once wrote in a position paper on restoring authority to the family here in the US:

> As a society becomes more complex, the family becomes even more essential as one place where a sense of trust, a degree of discipline, and a capacity of love can be nourished, and often as the only place where people are cherished because of who and what they are.

Anthropologist Margaret Mead once wrote: "Can we move to a firm belief that living in a family is worth great effort? Can we move to a new expectation that by making the effort families can endure?"

It is just that kind of commitment—broad-based and wide-ranging, but also deeply personal—that must happen if families are to survive and, ultimately, if society is to survive too.

Consider the circumstances of our children, the future as far as we can see.

Children

The child is father of the man, just as the poet said. That means the best way a society has of looking to the future is to look closely at its children today. A family's greatest contribution, of course, is in nurturing its children for productive roles in society at large. There is reason for concern.

In the US the numbers are shocking enough, though each culture has unique problems and numbers cannot tell the whole story of any culture:

• One million US children run away from home every year, making themselves vulnerable to exploitation;

Restoring Healthy Tradition

While healing often involves a battle against harmful traditions (see Chapter 5), it can also require just the opposite—getting back to long-forgotten or neglected basics after wandering off course. Some traditions seem to be built around fundamental human needs, such as the need for a loving family. As we enter the 1990s, the United Nations General Assembly has decided (thanks in large part to the efforts of one of this book's authors, Robert Muller, incidentally) to hold an International Year of the Family to honor this most basic of social systems.

Many individuals, cultures and subcultures this century have tried to replace the foundation of human society—the family—with alternative life styles such as communal living, living together as an unmarried couple, and joining charismatic organizations which attempt to pull individuals away from their families and to give the members the support and solidarity one normally receives from family. As much as we experiment with alternatives, nothing seems to fulfill our deepest inner needs as completely as a loving family. There seems to be a powerful need embedded deeply in our genetic make-up for intimate, loving bonds of two adults and their child(ren) all totally committed to each other for life.

—MHM

• Half of all abused children are under age 3;
• Half of all sex abusers are natural parents;
• One of every four children under age 6 lives in poverty;
• One-third of our current crop of 40 million school-age children have some strike against them when they enter school—poverty, broken home, minority status, non-English speaking;
• Teen suicide tripled in 30 years and infant homicides are up in the '80s;
• One-third of all children born today will spend some time in poverty before reaching adulthood;
• Of every 100 children born in 1983, twelve were born out of wedlock, 40 will live in a family where there is at least one divorce, five will experience a prolonged parental separation and two will experience the death of a parent;
• Poverty for children in the US is mostly the result of family breakdown; two of three children who entered poverty over the last decade and a half lived in single mother families. (A Los Angeles study shows that the first year after divorce, the average mother and children suffer a 73 percent decline in their standard of living. The National Science Foundation has calculated that divorce doubled the incidence of poverty among children.)

The numbers march on, but they lie. Not every runaway child is reported, every abused child known, every neglected child counted or the cry of every hungry child heard. It may be true that most children find love, protection and care in a nurturing family (of some configuration) but if any do not, isn't the problem just as real and the challenge just as great? These forgotten children cannot be expected to grow into productive, responsible adults easily. They need the attention of a caring society, a society that will fill a family's void or provide the support a family needs to make itself work. A report by the Metropolitan Court Judges of 1986—18 months in the making—pointed to the crucial role of the family and the importance of strengthening family values as more vital than law or social work in addressing the needs of children. The report's message: We must have a "rekindled commitment that the family is the foundation for the protection, care and training of our children."

The definition of childhood, of course, is culturally relative and historically whimsical. Are children chattel or cherished privilege? Are children willful, untamed savages, small adults, angelic creatures unsullied by greed, envy and the perversity of adulthood or are they individuals who have not yet matured and who need the nurturing of a caring society?

How do we keep families together? How do we prevent teen pregnancies? How do we save children from a cycle of abuse and neglect, ignorance and hopelessness? How do we guarantee for children the inalienable right to the pursuit of happiness? How do we come to some consensus on values worth sharing and strengthening? How do we help troubled children and at the same time respect family diversity and authority?

These are not questions easily answered, but if we are to get to the basics of society's ills, they are questions that can no longer be ignored.

Back to Family

Today's families have changed. At the same time, job structures have changed. The growth of low-wage, part-time work provides families with less income and often no health insurance or other essential benefits to meet their family needs. Families in which both parents work and families in which neither parent works and families in which only one parent is present—all require special and varied attention. But when only 30 percent of the 40-year-old professional women in the US have children, compared to Britain's 70 percent, something important is being suggested about the role of support like maternity leave and medical care. The new workforce realities create special realities for families. Consider that Japan offers 12 weeks of maternity leave at 60 percent salary, France offers 16 weeks at 90 percent and West Germany 14 weeks fully paid and wonder why we're still debating the issue of maternity leave in the US at all.

The American Family Celebration, a coalition spanning both major political parties, issued a recent resolution that warrants attention:

> In order to survive, all families must have affordable, quality support, including:
> - jobs and economic security,
> - health care,
> - child and elder care,
> - family leave,

- services for the elderly,
- quality education,
- equal opportunity,
- equal pay for work of equal value,
- shelter,
- a safe environment in which to live and work.

A national family policy must include provisions for child care, health care, elderly services, family and medical leave, equity in quality education, permanent housing, an end to discrimination, and economic justice.

We may not as a nation nor certainly as a world speak with one voice on the particular solutions to particular problems facing the family. There may not be one single agenda that will satisfy all our needs or alleviate all our concerns. But what we must have is a greater willingness to talk about family issues as public issues, and a recognition that the two cannot be separate and solved.

Families are under pressures not entirely of their own making. Families cannot be expected, then, to effect solutions all alone, in the privacy of their homes.

Getting back to basics of the family will require the efforts and energies of a united and caring nation within an increasingly united and caring world.

Part II:
Healing Our Societies

Healing families are those whose members are opening their hearts. Communication channels are opening up perhaps by such means as weekly family meetings and open discussion of problems. Everyone's needs are being met, especially the needs of children for discipline and unconditional love. While these changes are taking place within the healing family, the family as a system is forming warm, responsible bonds with the larger groups of which it is part—the neighborhood, perhaps a church or religious group, the school which the kids attend. So, for a family to be in a genuine healing mode, there must be healing going on within it and around it. That is true of any social group—a club, a company, a church, a city or whatever: being "healthy" involves internal and external efforts.

A healing society must be an amazing thing to envision. A rekindling of love within families and neighborliness throughout cities as people become concerned about the conditions and future of their communities. In the western world, businesses would shift their raison d'etre from making money to nurturing healthy, happy employees and environmentally conscious, community-responsible policies. They would be run more from the heart.

Liang Jimin and Wang Xiangying show how the Chinese family fits into a highly integrated social structure. The Chinese people seem to share a culture-wide heart bond missing from most western societies, a bond which hones the people's intuition and creates a common mind, allowing massive trends and movements to sweep across the country.

Paul Wachtel delves into the myth that a rapidly growing society is a healthy society. Our obsession for more-more-more may simply be hiding the western world's unmet needs for love and community.

Majid Rahnema describes a movement underway today in India that is healing large segments of society as it brings self-realization and a deep sense of community to a swelling cross-section of the population.

Joseph Schaeffer interviews five of the world's great minds to get an idea of what our children would need today to build a healthy, happy world for their children to grow up in.

Chapter Five:
Family Planning in China

by Dr. Liang Jimin and
Wang Xiangying

Their background. Leading officials in the China's family planning program. Dr. Liang, vice president of the China Family Planning Association, teaches Medicine and Population Studies at Hebei University and holds numerous administrative and editorial posts in associations dealing with population, demographics and eugenics. He has practiced medicine and has served as a public official in health, culture and education since 1948. Ms. Wang, division chief of the State Family Planning Commission of China, is involved with numerous international seminars, committees, conferences, articles and books, mostly on the subjects of family planning, economics and international relations.

Their chapter. China has been rocked in recent history by political upheaval and policy changes that have swept across the country like a typhoon, completely transforming the values of the people. Today the political and economic policy is clear: Modernize society, educate the people and, above all, get a handle on population growth. This fascinating chapter explores the history, the obstacles and the future of China's unique circumstances.

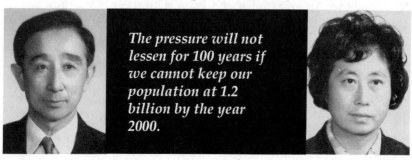

The pressure will not lessen for 100 years if we cannot keep our population at 1.2 billion by the year 2000.

Family Planning in China

by Dr. Liang Jimin and Wang Xiangying

Our understanding of population planning strategy and China's unique population growth pattern under the socialist system have been taking shape in the repeated process of "practice-knowledge-practice." China's family planning program has experienced a lot of twists and turns in the past 30 years. It was not until 1978, after the country shifted its focus to economic construction, that family planning guidelines became clear and policy was improved. Since then political commitment from leaders at various levels has strengthened and effective measures have been adopted to implement the program. The whole society has been mobilized as publicity and education have raised people's awareness. As a result, the concept of small family size is taking deep root in people's minds along with the desire for socio-economic development and improved living standards.

More and more people are voluntarily practicing contraception. China's rapid population growth has been brought under control as the transition is underway from blind growth to planned growth. Practice has proved that it is both possible and necessary to promote family planning in China. There is no doubt now that our strategy to solve our population problem is the correct one and is ideally suited to China's specific conditions.

1949-59—Economic Reconstruction

For three years after the founding of the People's Republic in 1949, the stage was set for rapid population growth. China entered an enthusiastic period of economic reconstruction. The population grew in an unplanned way while the death rate dropped drastically. The national economy grew fast, and a large labor force was badly needed for the construction.

Researchers working on population theory began to think that rapid growth was a sign of prosperity and thus was an inevitable objective law for socialist countries. Abortion was put under strict government control. Sterilization was prohibited.

The Uphill Fight Against Harmful Tradition

Healing is often an uphill fight against habit and tradition. On the personal side it may involve adopting more wholesome attitudes towards eating and exercise—giving up harmful things we've grown accustomed to, such as high-fat foods, excessive sweets, and addictive substances like caffeine, nicotine and alcohol. In society it may involve changing age-old customs or widely held beliefs that were fine in the past but now present a threat. While the overdeveloped West struggles to reconcile a heritage of abundance and carefree consumption in a modern world of vanishing resources and spreading environmental destruction, many Third World countries are finding some success grappling with a population compelled by a tradition of large families to burgeon and outstrip supplies of food and resources.

Reducing excessive population to manageable levels does not happen quickly except through such catastrophes as famine, war and mass execution. Sensible birth control policies take time, but the pay-off is good. The Japanese in the 1950s reduced population growth to about 1 percent per year and have emerged in the later decades of this century as a leader in world industry and technology. Other once-struggling East Asian nations have enjoyed similar economic rewards. Singapore and Hong Kong cut their population growth rates in half during the 60s, and today are following on the heels of Japan in world trade. If poor countries were to enact effective policies now, in the last decade of this century, presumedly they would begin feeling economic vitality early next milennium, at which time they could begin developing their social structures to sustainable blueprints now being drawn up by leading-edge thinkers on all continents. That is where China, a sprawling nation comprising one-fifth of the world's population, is apparently headed.

We are emerging from the age of human rights to a new age of balance between human rights, social system rights, ecosystem rights, and world rights. If everyone wants more—more material goods, more children, more property, and bigger homes—as part of their human rights, then a policy of freedom and democracy could easily destroy the world environment. There must grow a balance between the rights of individuals, groups, and the world as a whole. China today seems to be seeking that balance.

—MHM

But the economic imbalances caused by unplanned population growth became obvious in no time and were brought to the attention of government leaders and scholars. Consequently, some changes took place in government policy.

• In August 1953, the State Council approved "Abortion and Contraceptive Methods," a policy submitted by the Ministry of Public Health legalizing birth control and abortion.

• In the "National Program of Agricultural Development" formulated under the personal supervision of late Chairman Mao Zedong, it was stipulated that "in all the densely-populated areas, family planning should be publicized, and birth control advocated. It is encouraged to bear a child in a planned way so as to relieve excess burden on the family and ensure better education and employment for individuals."

• In 1956, Premier Zhou Enlai stated in the Proposal for the Second Five-Year-Plan of National Economic Development that "to protect women and children, to ensure good education for future generations and to make our nation healthy and prosperous, we should advocate proper control of childbearing."

• In 1957, Chairman Mao Zedong added, "Human beings should control their fertility and sustain population growth in a planned way. . . . A ten-year-plan is needed for birth planning."

• At the same time, Mr. Ma Yinchu, the well-known economist, published his book, "New Theory on Population," advocating population control in China.

• Education and popularizing of contraceptive information were carried out in cities above the county level, and family planning guidance was made available. A pilot family planning program was started in some cities.

However, in early 1958, the pendulum swung. Mr. Ma Yinchu and other scholars sharing his viewpoint of promoting birth control were wantonly repudiated. As a result the population policy, demographic research, education for birth control and the implementation of a family planning program all came to a standstill. Little progress was made during this period. The average annual increase of China's population from 1955-1959 remained as high as 2.2 percent.

The Struggle of the Sixties

The period of 1959-1961 was the most difficult period in China's economic development history. The population growth rate drastically went down. In 1962, the growth rate went up again, by a big margin, to 3.35 percent, reaching the biggest birth rise seen in China since 1949. Facing this new population momentum, the idea of birth planning was once again put forward. In 1962, in the "Directive on Earnestly Advocating Family Planning," issued by the Chinese government, it was stipulated that family planning should be promoted in cities and densely-populated rural areas. It is an established policy in the course of socialist construction that population natural growth rate should be under control and turn unplanned childbearing to planned childbearing. To materialize this purpose, pilot family planning projects were sponsored in urban areas and great efforts were made for contraceptive research and service delivery. Beginning in 1964, the birth rate in urban areas began to drop. Unfortunately, this didn't last long. The so-called Great Cultural Revolution (The Ten-Year Turmoil) swept everything away, including the family planning program. From 1966 to 1974, China's population kept on increasing at a high rate with an average number of 26 million births a year, and a net increase of 20 million a year. The year 1968 was the peak year with 27.57 million newborns. The 250 million new people born during the 10 years from 1966 to 1976 constituted a second "baby boom" in China.

The implications of imbalance between growth of material production and population became obvious. In the 1950s, the 4 million unemployed workers left over from the old China were properly arranged for and their basic needs satisfied. In the 1970s, however, unemployment became a problem in China again as 10 million urban young people became jobless.

Popularization of Family Planning

Since the 1970s thanks to advocation by the late Chairman Mao Zedong and the tremendous efforts made by the late Premier Zhou Enlai, family planning management groups were set up at central and provincial levels and family planning offices were established in existing health sectors. After 1973, population planning was joined with national economic planning, and a policy of planned population growth was formulated. Hence, a state-guided population control movement unfolded throughout the whole country.

The basic elements of the policy were late birth, good spacing and fewer births. It was advocated that the best family size was one child per couple, with two children maximum. For national minorities, "proper measures should be taken to increase population and develop production. However, guidance and service should be rendered to those who have too many children and ask for contraception." During this period of time, the family planning program made great strides. As a result, the annual average birth rate dropped from 3.31 percent between 1966 and 1970 down to 2.4 percent in 1978.

Family Planning Today

The Third Session of the 11th National Congress of the Chinese Communist Party shifted the country's focus on economic development and thus opened up new vistas for the socialist modernization program. With this new focus, the family planning program turned over a new page both in theory and in practice. In the past decade, population control through family planning has been identified as a strategic issue with importance throughout the whole process of socio-economic development. Directives and statements from the Central Committee of the Chinese Communist Party and the State Council made clear the guidelines for implementing the family planning program, with explicit population targets. Specific policy and measures were all stipulated. To practice family planning was identified as one of the basic state policies of China.

Since 1980, China has advocated one child for one couple with exceptions for those rural couples that have actual difficulties in having only one child. They can have another child with good spacing. However, under no circumstances should they have a third child. By 1982, the population policy was amended explicitly "to limit the size of the population and improve its quality." Specifically, "later marriage, late childbearing, fewer births and healthy births" was promoted. Meanwhile regulations for incentives and disincentives were also worked out.

Legal grounds were also made available for family planning in the country. In the National Constitution, it is stipulated that "the state promotes family planning" and "the purpose of practicing family planning is to make the population growth commensurate with socio-economic development." The National Marriage Law also stipulates that "both husband and wife are duty bound to practice family planning."

In summary, the last decade saw a drastic decline in our population. China's family planning program has had remarkable effects on our society.

CHINA'S POPULATION STRATEGY AND POLICY

The guidelines in formulating the strategy and policy are to have, first of all, thorough understanding and analysis of the unique conditions in China. Based on our many years of practice, a population strategy has been tailored to best suit China's specific conditions.

Rationales for China's Population Strategy and Policy

Socialist objectives. China is undergoing socialist construction under the leadership of the Chinese Communist Party. Based on the public ownership of production materials and according to the objective law of socialist economy and population growth, China is promoting a commodity economy while regulating human reproduction, all in a planned way, in order to make population growth and socio-economic development mutually compatible.

The overall purpose and target of economic development is to quadruple the gross industrial and agricultural output value, to raise the people's material and cultural living standards to a higher level, and to put China, by mid 21st century, among middle ranking developed countries. To meet this ambitious goal, it is imperative to keep China's population growth under control, to improve its quality and to regulate its structure. For all these purposes, a good strategy is vital.

A large, fast-growing population. By the end of 1987, the total population on the mainland reached 1,080.73 million representing 21 percent of the world total. It doubled the total of 541.67 million in 1949. In terms of the total population, it took every five odd years from 1964 to 1981 to increase 100 million (from 700 million in 1964 to one billion in 1981) with an elapse of only 17 years. Since 1978, thanks to the family planning program, the growth rate has slowed down noticeably. From 1981 to 1985, there was an average annual increase of 11.65 million only. However, starting from 1986, China has entered into another birth and marriage peak which will last for a dozen years. The 360 million people born during the second baby boom from 1962 to 1975, an average of 25.80 million a year, are now stepping into the age of marriage and childbearing. From now on, every year, 11 million couples will enter into marriage and reproductive age.

Demographic problems. Our current population structure has a number of serious problems:

• We are in transition from a young population to an adult one, which will apply economic pressure on our society for the next 35 years.

• We have more males than females (30.69 million more in 1982, for example), an imbalance that has unfavorable impact on marriage, family, reproduction, migration and population composition.

• Our population is unevenly distributed in geographic terms, with 97 percent of the population residing in the Southeast and Northeast parts of China, which accounts for less than half of the land area. This will inevitably result in an imbalance between the processing and manufacturing industry, and the energy and mining industry. Only by regulating the geographic distribution of the population and developing the Northwest and Southwest China, can the imbalanced industrial structure be improved.

• China has too big a proportion of rural population—too few people in the cities. In 1981, only 29 percent of the people in developed countries lived in rural areas, compared to 73.2 percent in developing countries. In China, 79.4 percent lived in rural areas in 1982.

Great potential but still underdeveloped. China's economy is advancing smoothly, and has a lot of potential. The large population provides a rich labor force. However, compared with modern developed countries, China's economy is still underdeveloped. Productivity remains at a low level. Manual labor is still commonplace in rural China, especially in mountainous areas where life is still very hard. Under these circumstances, the high growth rate of population inevitably puts pressure on clothing, food, housing, transportation, education and employment. Even with recent increases in grain production, education and transportation facilities, if it is calculated per capita wise, with such a big population, China is still far behind many other countries. After the reform of the rural economic system, many farmers still have some difficulties in their household economy, everyday life and doing income-generating work with big families. The overall purpose is to make population control serve the objectives of socio-economic development and people's aspiration for improving the quality of their lives.

Intelligent but undereducated population. China is a country with an ancient civilization and long, rich history. The Chinese people are traditionally intelligent, hardworking and courageous. However, China also has a long history of hardships and misery. Traditional, outmoded ideas are still lingering in many people's minds. The population is therefore less developed in terms of education, culture, modern science and technology. According to the 1982 national census, only 0.6 percent of the total population received higher education, 6.6 percent high school education, 17.8 percent junior middle school education and 35.8 percent primary school education. These percent–ages are far below the level of many other countries. For example, the proportion of population with high education is 14.9 percent in the US, 12 percent in Canada, 6.4 percent in Japan, 4.5 percent in the USSR, 2.3 percent in Yugoslavia and 1.0 percent in Brazil. There are 235.82 million illiterates and semi-literates (those who can read 500-1500 Chinese characters but still cannot fully understand newspapers) accounting for 23.5 percent of the total population, and 31.9 percent of the total population of 12 years and over.

There are only 3.143 million health professionals. Among them, 777 thousand are medical doctors (including doctors of traditional medicine, excluding para-medicals) with a ratio of 0.73 doctors per 10 thousand people, as against 3.46 in the USSR, 2.04 in Federal Republic of Germany, 1.68 in the US, 1.65 in Poland, 1.18 in Japan and 0.92 in Egypt. The physical quality of China's population can by no means satisfy the need of the modernization program. Among the newborns every year, there are 2-4 percent with birth defects totaling 400-800 thousand a year.

It is estimated that over 1 percent of the population, or 15 million people, are to some degree physically and mentally handicapped. About 1.5 million children are mentally retarded, representing 0.5 percent of the national total. China's infant mortality rate was 34.68 percent in 1981, still much higher than that of developed countries. The age-specific mortality rate for the middle and aged population is generally higher than that of the US, Japan, Switzerland. . . . The physical development indicators for 7- to 25-year-olds in terms of height, weight, and chest circumference, are far less favorable than that of some European countries.

Abundant resources, but hardly enough to go around. China has rich natural resources, but not if calculated per capita-wise. China is the third largest country while the average per capita area is only 1/30th of the world average.

China is far below the world average in per capita arable land, forests and grassland. China has only 2700 cubic meters of water per person while the world average is 11,000 cubic meters. In North China, more than 100 million people do not have enough water. In the remote mountainous areas and pastures, more than 20 million people still lack drinking water.

Cultural imbalance. China has 56 nationalities with the Han nationality being the clear majority. The 55 minorities represent only 6.7 percent of the country's total population. It has been the state's consistent policy to promote the economy and population growth among the minorities with full respect for their customs and life style.

Opening to the world. China is pursuing a policy of opening to the outside world. This provides a favorable environment for foreign investment, advanced technology and experience to improve our own work.

These are the basic facts about China's present situation that are being taken into account as we formulate our population strategies.

Strategies Toward the Year 2000

The objective of China's modernization program is to continually satisfy the increasing demand of the people for material and cultural life by upgrading productivity. This will require limiting the growth of the population, improving its quality, and adjusting its composition. We shall strive hard to keep our population at around 1.2 billion by the year 2000.

Limiting the size. It is recorded in Chinese history that our population has been stable during most of the past 2,000 years. There were 59.59 million Chinese in AD 2, and 60 million in AD 1393. It was during the Qing Dynasty, from about 1650 to 1850, that population exploded. It crossed the first 100 million mark by the year 1685, the second 100 million by 1764 and the fourth 100 million by 1849. It was the first great leap forward in China's population history and thus laid a large base for the population. The second leap forward took place in the 38 years after the founding of the Republic from 1949 to 1987 when population was doubled from 542 million to 1080 million. During this period, China's population grew at a similar speed and a bit higher than world population growth.

The 1990s are decisive to the success of our population control program. It is estimated that since 1970 the family planning program has averted 200 million unwanted births. However, another birth peak period already started in 1986 as 360 million young adults born during the period from 1962 to 1975 are entering the age of marriage and childbearing, and the actively reproductive women of 20-24 years old are increasing year by year. From 1987, every year almost 13 million women have been entering marriage and childbearing age, and will not decline to 9 million until the end of this century.

As a result, China's birth rate rose from 1.78 percent in 1985 to 2.08 percent in 1986 and 2.1 percent in 1987, and higher still in 1988. We expect this high birth rate and high natural increase rate to last until 1995 before slowing down gradually. By 2000 the natural growth rate will possibly decline to 1 percent.

If we are successful, the average annual births will have been 22 million between 1988 and 1995, and 18 million from 1996 to 2000. The combined total of newborns during the 13 years will be 266 million. With the deduction of around 106 million deaths the net increase will be 160 million. Plus the 1080 million in 1987, the total population of China's mainland will be around 1240 million. Thus it is hopeful that the population will be stabilized at 1300-1400 million by the middle of next century.

If we fail in our work or make policy mistakes, it is still possible that the population will reach 1300 million by the end of this century and 1500 million by 2050. In that case, all our previous efforts will be half ruined, the stabilization of the population will be postponed, and our plans for economic construction will fall short. Only with consistency and redoubled efforts by all departments can we fulfill our objectives.

Economic construction. To realize the long term objective of our national economic construction, we are following a three-step plan:

• To double the gross national output value of production as of 1980, and eliminate the problem of food and clothing shortages.

• To double the 1988 national production output value by the end of this century and raise people's living standard to a well-off level. ·

• To make the GNP per capita reach the level of middle-developed countries so people live comfortable lives and the country is basically modernized.

The first step has been reached, and we are now in the process of the second step. It is estimated that by the year 2000, our GNP will amount to 1180 billion US dollars. If calculated on the basis of 1.25 billion population by then, the GNP per capita will reach 950 US dollars.

In case we fail in our population control target, it will not only reduce the GNP per capita, but also take away some investment for capital construction to cover additional expenditures resulting from excessive births. Should the total population reach or surpass 1.3 billion, the target for the second step will not be met and the rank of China in the world in terms of GNP per capita will be far down on the list. If our population cannot be checked, the grave pressure will not be lessened within the coming 100 years. In conclusion, we should say that to keep our population at around 1.2 billion by the year 2000 is a vital strategy of far-reaching significance.

Promoting a quality population. Poor physical condition combined with low educational attainment constantly brings about a relatively high birth rate. Among those women with multiple birth (more than two children) in 1981, those with primary school education accounted for 26.1 percent; with junior middle school education, 9.22 percent; with senior middle school education, 5.3 percent; and with higher education, 1.6 percent. This composition of education levels makes for an unfavorable situation in China. Therefore, it is vital that we quickly upgrade the quality of our population through education.

By the year 2000, the government will try to eradicate illiteracy among people under 50 years of age by popularizing primary and middle school education. If it is realized, the rate of illiteracy in the population will drop from 23.5 to 5 percent, while the proportion of people with higher education will reach 2.0.

In terms of physical quality, we hope that by the year 2000, the incidence rate of malformed children will decrease from the current 3 percent of the total children born to about 1 percent, thus averting 200,000 to 400,000 births of mentally retarded children. We project infant mortality will decrease from 3.5 percent in 1981 to 2 percent, while life expectancy increases from 68.9 in 1985 to 72.

Adjusting population structure. By the year 2000 we mean to be well underway toward ideal age composition, sex ratio, ratio between urban and rural population and an even geographic distribution.

• Age composition. As mentioned earlier, China is now in a transition from a young population to an adult one. By the year 2000 we expect that the proportion of juveniles age 0 to 14 will drop from its current 33.5 percent to 22 percent or so, the population aged 15 to 64 will rise from 55.9 percent to around 70 percent, and that of population above 65 years old will increase from 4.9 percent to about 7 percent. Around the year 2024 China's aging population will attain the high level of 16 percent occurring today in some countries. After that the aging process will slow down.

• Sex ratio. Since 1949, China's population has remained about 51.5 percent male, 48.5 percent female. We hope to correct this imbalance which is caused by, first, a legacy of imbalanced sex ratio from Old China; second, a comparatively high sex ratio of newborns; third, a comparatively small difference of mortality between the two sexes; and fourth, a problem of either too high or too low sex ratios between cities and countryside and among different regions primarily as a result of population mobility.

• Population distribution. Urban population rose from 20 percent of China's total population in 1982 to 22.13 percent in

1986, but is still lower than that of all developed countries and most developing countries. This is now being corrected quickly as people move to the cities and towns from rural areas, with the reform of the urban economic structure and fast development of the rural economy, particularly the prosperity of the commodity economy in the countryside. It is reckoned that the proportion of total population in cities and towns will rise to about 38.0 percent by the year 2000, most of the flow going to towns rather than cities.

The regional population imbalance will develop without any fundamental changes—high density in the eastern part of China and sparsity in the western part.

China's Family Planning Policy Today

The overall goal of China's family planning policy is to limit the size of the population, improve its quality, and to keep population growth commensurate with socio-economic development, utilization of resources and environment, and above all, to strive to limit population size at around 1.2 billion by the end of the century. Such a general policy may be divided into policies on birth, on incentives and disincentives, and on technology.

Birth policy. The birth policy is to advocate late marriage and late childbearing, fewer but better births, and one child for one couple. Moreover, with certain exceptions under special circumstances, one child per couple is promoted among government and state-owned enterprise employees and urban residents. Families in the rural areas with real difficulties and wishing to have a second child, including those whose first child is a girl, may have another child after an interval of several years. They should not have third births under any circumstances. Family planning is also advocated among minorities. Nevertheless, regulations and specific requirements are to be worked out by provinces and autonomous regions concerned, based on local circumstances.

According to China's Marriage Law, the earliest legal marriage age is 22 for a man and 20 for a woman. "Later marriage" refers to a 3-year postponement from the legal marriage age. "Later childbearing," then, is by married women aged 25 and over.

Later marriage and later childbearing result in better births. According to a survey conducted by the State Family Planning Commission on newborns with birth defects in 23 counties, children who were born when their mothers were 23 to 30 years old enjoy a low death rate and best possible physique.

Better births refer to children with well developed intelligence and good health. Births with mental retardation, mental disorders and other birth defects that hinder people from managing their own lives, and that are brought about by hereditary and congenital diseases, should be prevented.

To advocate fewer births is primarily designated to limit population size. The government is now vigorously promoting the practice of one child per couple, and is making efforts to raise the proportion of single children among the newborns.

Conditions under which a second birth may be arranged are specified by each province, autonomous region or municipality based on local circumstances. For government and state-owned enterprise employees, one regulation provides preferential considerations for a second birth to couples:

• whose first child has a non-congenital disease that will prevent him or her from doing normal work,

• who are themselves the only children in their respective families,

• who get pregnant after five years' infertility after marriage with one adopted child, or

• who are married again and have not had any unplanned births on both sides during the last marriage.

Regulations vary from province to province on second birth to couples who live in rural areas and face real difficulties. A majority of provinces arrange a planned second birth to couples having only a female child and upon their own request, with a birth interval of several years. Specific justifications for a second child are formulated by local authorities.

Incentives and disincentives. Adhering voluntarily to the family planning guidelines is the honorable way to live in China today, and honor is important to the Chinese people. Education and encouragement are mostly responsible for the participative attitude prevalent throughout most of the country. Incentives also play an important part. Disincentives are used when necessary.

Current moral incentives mainly include conferring honorary certificates and honorary titles to families and parents that follow government's call to have only one child. Economic incentives include single-child health subsidies, or allowances for parents, or allocation of more farmland or a larger share of profits. Single-child mothers enjoy longer maternal leave, and the families in the countryside are assisted in finding ways to improve their income while enjoying priority consideration in kindergarten and school enrollment, medical care, employment and training opportunities, housing, etc.

Disincentives primarily refer to economic restrictions on couples having unplanned births, in an effort to compensate the social investment on unplanned children and to promote voluntary acceptance of family planning. Specifically, such couples are fined, or allocated less farmland but are required to contribute more funds. They are deprived of the social welfare enjoyed by families with a reasonable number of children. The couples will also receive certain administrative punishments if they are members of the Chinese Communist Party or Youth League, or employees of government and state-owned enterprises.

Government officials who cheat or engage in malpractices for personal gains in this field are criticized, and criminal prosecution is conducted on those who disrupt the practice of family planning in such ways as conducting operation of illegal abortions and the removal of IUDs, abandoning infants, abusing and discriminating against mothers who give birth to daughters, attacking and revenging family planning workers, encroaching citizens' legal rights and interests in family planning, and so on.

In Old China, many children meant more security in old age. Today the same care is available to the aged regardless of whether they are childless or have only children away. The childless aged may live collectively, at their own will, in the "Homes of Respect for the Aged" where houses are provided and full-time employees are assigned, by village committee, to look after and provide medical care to the elderly. Those living separately are basically cared for and supported by their relatives or employees sent by a village committee. Their daily sustenance and medical care are equally guaranteed.

Policy on technology. The principle behind implementing a family planning program in China is to advocate comprehensive means of contraception, such as temporary, permanent and remedial means. Couples can select the contraceptive measures they prefer. Temporary or short-acting measures include pills, injectables, condoms and others. Permanent or long-acting choices are vasectomy, occlusion male sterilization, minilap and occlusion female sterilization, IUD, norplant, etc. Remedial means refers to voluntary abortions after failure in contraception. Abortion should only be exercised in prescribed procedures in qualified institutions and the quality of the operation must be ensured. In China all contraceptives and birth control operations are provided free of charge by the State. All contraceptives are manufactured by China's over thirty factories with products of over twenty kinds in six categories and with an annual output that serves over 40 million persons yearly.

Multi-level policy. China's family planning policy incorporates the interests of the State, communities and individuals. It provides sweeping standards while allowing flexible decisions by the local authorities to meet their specific needs. It also incorporates State guidance with people's voluntary participation. The State works out unified laws and policies and motivates people to participate voluntarily through publicity and education and provision of free contraceptive services. The government adheres to the principle of voluntary participation and is absolutely opposed to coercion of any kind.

Putting Family Planning into Practice

Implementing a sensible family planning policy with growing success has involved these steps:

Adhering to family planning as a basic State policy. The population issue has always been important in China's socio-economic development. The government has put intensive emphasis on the issue and considers it a long term strategic one. The national Constitution and Marriage Law have special stipulations for family planning. Deng Xiaoping, the senior leader in China, pointed out that we fought for decades just for eradication of poverty, and the practice of family planning will make China prosper at a faster speed. Zhao Ziyang, the General Secretary of CPC, emphasized that we need two basic national policies to ensure success in our modernization program: 1) to develop productivity wholeheartedly and stick to the general principle of reform and opening up to the outside world, and 2) to keep population growth under control and upgrade its quality. At present, the guidelines, birth policy and population target are designed to serve and ensure the realization of overall socio-economic development.

Strictly carrying out the policy. The family planning policy is implemented while considering socio-economic development strategies, the current population situation and people's childbearing wishes. Such a policy has been gradually perfected over a long period of time and has played a significant role in stemming the fast population growth characteristic of China in recent centuries. Statistics show that by the end of 1987, single children numbered 32.3 million. Among married couples in the country, those who want to have only one child account for 16.2 percent, and over 90 percent of the couples having one child in cities have applied for single child certificates. Since nearly 80 percent of China's people live in the countryside, family planning work in the rural areas has always been the focus. The past decade witnessed a reasonable and effective policy that has indeed checked the rapid increase of population and brought about a close relationship between the government and the people. Such a policy therefore should be consistent and stable for a long time.

Spreading the word and means. The purpose of publicity and education service is to offer information on policies, population science and theories and knowledge for healthy birth and better childraising. Education helps people gradually change their concepts of family, parenting and child value. Technical services include delivery of contraceptives and counseling on childbearing and maternal and child health. New ways and means for fertility control are under research for a greater degree of effectiveness, safety, convenience and economy.

Refining the social network. In China everyone is related to family planning directly or indirectly. This work can be done only with social support. A complete network touching virtually every Chinese household has greatly ensured smooth implementation of the program. This network is composed of three channels.

• The government channel covers family planning commissions and departments concerned in the government at levels from central down to county. Organizations at grassroot levels such as villages, neighborhoods, factories, etc. all designate professional or part time family planning workers. China now has over 140,000 full time family planning workers plus more than one million part-time workers.

• The second channel includes institutions for publicity and contraceptive services, population research and studies, statistics and information.

• The third channel involves non-governmental organizations like the China Family Planning Association, China Women's Federation, Trade Union and Population Society, Communist Youth League, etc. These departments and organizations work together to ensure the smooth implementation of the population policy.

Concerted efforts for success. How has China, with a backward economy and low level of science and culture, achieved such a dramatic decline of fertility? It is a breakthrough of the population problem both in concept and in practice. The Chinese Party and government have paid exceptional attention to our population program. Meanwhile, the leading and exemplary role of Party and Youth League members and activists is valuable. They not only practice family planning themselves, but also lead, organize and help people to remove their difficulties and apprehensions about the program. As family planning is a huge project involving people from all walks of life, the whole society has to be mobilized. Working together we can be sure that our family planning program will enjoy continuing success.

Achievements of Family Planning

Within the decade from 1978 to 1988, remarkable achievements have been made in family planning work under the leadership of the Central Committee of the Chinese Communist Party and the State Council. The birth rate and natural growth rate have dropped considerably and population growth has been under effective control.

Considerable fertility decline. By the end of 1987, the total population of China's mainland reached 1080.73 million as a result of the birth rate decline from 3.4 percent in the 1960s to 2.5 percent in the 1970s, and further to 1.8 percent in the last nine years. If calculated on the basis of the fertility level in 1970, a total population of 200 million has been averted within the 17 years from 1971 to 1987. This has primarily lessened the imbalance between fast population growth and socio-economic development. The average Chinese woman had 5.87 children in the 1950s, 5.68 in the 1960s, 4.01 in the 1970s, 2.24 in the 1980s, 2.63 in 1981, 2.48 in 1982, 2.07 in 1983, 2.0 in 1984, 2.2 in 1985, and 2.4 in 1986 and 1987.

Later marriages. The average age of first marriage of Chinese women was 18.46 in the 1940s, 19.02 in the 1950s, 19.81 in the 1960s, 21.59 in the 1970s and was further increased in the last decade.

Increase in contraceptive use. In 1981, 105 million people (64.4 percent of married couples of reproductive age) practiced contraception and birth control. By 1988, 155 million (77.3 percent) did.

More planned births. The rate of planned births has increased from 65.1 percent in 1979 to 74.2 percent in 1983 and the upward trend continues now.

Extensive research into contraception methods. Based on the research priority for contraceptives and means of fertility control, during the 6th Five Year Plan from 1981 to 1985, 21 significant research results at the national level and 48 results at the ministerial level were accomplished. They are, among others, study on efficacy of IUD, female long-acting contraceptives, occlusion male sterilization, etc.

Breakthroughs in birth and child care. Remarkable progress has been made in popularizing new delivery methods and providing maternal and child health care. The average maternal mortality rate has dropped from 1.5 percent before 1949 to 0.05 percent and infant mortality rate has declined from 20 percent before 1949 to 3.5 percent in 1981, and to 1.8 percent in some cities and 3 percent in some counties in 1987. The average life expectancy reached 68.9 in 1985 with 71 for women and 67 for men. The health conditions of Chinese women and children are greatly improved. The physique, moral standard and cultural attainment of young people are also upgraded.

Changing attitudes. Development of socio-economy, culture and science, improvement of people's living standards as well as extensive family planning education have jointly brought about a change in the traditional concept of "more sons, more blessings" in the following aspects:

• Small family norm is taking root in many people's minds. The average number of children per couple is declining from 5-6 in the 1960s, and 4 in the 1970s to 2.3 in the 1980s According to a survey conducted by Liaoning Province among 702 people in three cities, 25.2 percent of urban and 8.7 percent of rural respondents indicated that they only want to have one child. Those who wished to have two children accounted for 74.4 percent in urban areas and 88.9 percent in rural areas while only 0.4 percent of urban and 2.4 percent of rural respondents wished to have three children.

• More and more people would rather have few but better mentally developed children. Parents attach great importance to education and mental development of their children even if they have to pay a lot for this purpose.

• People became very willing to observe the birth planning regulations by having one or two children only and to give up their own wish for more children.

A survey among 570 parents of single children in Zigong City, Sichuan Province, indicated that those who want to have only one child all their lives, account for 66 percent of people with higher education, 43 percent of the workers and 15.14 percent of the farmers. Those who want two children are 1 percent of the people with higher education, 9 percent of the workers and 41.35 percent of the farmers. No one wished to have three children.

• People are eager to be informed of basic science to guide their marriage and childbearing.

• Along with the development of commodity economy, people tend to devote all their spare energy to income-generating projects rather than to childraising. At the same time, as the cost of raising a child is increasing and the old age support system is improving, the value of a child in a family is changed.

We can only conclude that China's population policy is correct and the program is effective. The population program is warmly accepted and participated in by the people and therefore is very successful.

Chapter Six:
Healing Our Social Neurosis

by Dr. Paul Wachtel

His background. Author of *The Poverty of Affluence.* Distinguished professor of Psychology at City College, New York, and an internationally recognized expert on integrative approaches to psychotherapy. Speaker and workshop leader for colleges, churches, synagogues and community groups. Writes social criticism for "The Nation" and "The New Republic."

His chapter. The security provided by a sense of community has largely vanished in the industrialized world. Are we trying in vain to compensate with growth and affluence? This chapter explains why the quest for more and more material goods is unsatisfying, and how this pursuit, elevated to a national obsession, creates global conflict, ecological devastation, and personal unhappiness. The solution: A way of life that can reverse the vicious cycles that drive us to produce, buy, and pollute at an ever-increasing rate in a vain quest of illusory substitutes for meaning and relatedness.

Our craving for possessions is an effort to compensate for something deep and basic that is missing from our lives.

Healing Our Social Neurosis

by Dr. Paul L. Wachtel

Symptoms of severe disorder abound in our society. Our air is unhealthy, our water increasingly in danger of contamination; toxins build up in our lakes, rivers, and even backyards; the ozone layer is depleting; acid rain renders lifeless waters once teeming with life; the Greenhouse Effect threatens the delicate biological balance; the gap between rich and poor is increasing; homeless people are sleeping in the streets; we have a growing underclass and a widening scourge of drugs and crime. It should take little for anyone with his or her eyes open to see that all is not well. It is not morning in America, but the morning after, and we are suffering from much more than just a hangover.

But if it's clear that something is wrong, it is less clear exactly what the disorder is or how to cure it. One must be cautious in making analogies between the ills of a society and those of an individual—it is essential that we be clear that they are analogies, and that we not take them too literally. If we follow these cautions, however, there may well be much that is useful in seeking to explore these analogies and to seek a "cure" to our society's ills.

The Addicted Society?

One model of our difficulties that suggests itself is that of addiction. In our society, as in the other industrial societies of the world that have organized themselves around the principle of growth—and hence around the expectation of always more, more, more—we are plagued by intense cravings. For many individuals in our society, the desire for more money and more material goods has a compulsive quality. And though our purchases are able to provide us with a "fix" in the short term, a momentary jolt that makes things seem better, they yield little in the way of long-term satisfaction. Rather, what they yield is simply momentary relief from the craving itself, and the craving is almost instantly regenerated after the immediate fix wears off.

Are We Victims of Overdose?

A related analogy that also is suggestive is that of overdose. We not only consume compulsively, even addictively, we also consume such quantities that we cause ourselves serious, perhaps even potentially fatal, damage. The most obvious damage is to the environment. I have already alluded to a number of troubling environmental trends at the very beginning of this chapter, and it is unfortunately the case that I only scratched the surface in that already ominous list. One need only think of the unwanted expansion of our knowledge of geography that has come through our involuntary acquaintance with such places as Love Canal, Three Mile Island, Bhopal, Chernobyl, or Valdez, Alaska.

But there is damage as well to the social fabric. The very fact of all the wealth that our society produces makes the absence of wealth even more intolerable. We have created a society in which people who live at a standard that once would have seemed perfectly adequate now feel deprived and left out. With our eye constantly on whether the economy is growing, we have failed to attend to how that growth is distributed. We have attempted to avoid dealing directly with the social disorder of inequality by trying instead to rely on the medicine of growth. We have assumed that if the pie is growing, those who are getting the smallest pieces won't notice; as long as their piece is bigger each year, that's all that matters. But people's perceptions are inherently comparative, our notions of what is adequate and of what is ample depend on what others around us have. If we have less than everyone else around us, we will not feel pleased even if what we have is "a lot."

There is considerable evidence for this view of how we perceive. Even simple studies by experimental psychologists of people making judgments of things like the weight of lifted objects show how deeply comparisons enter into our experience of the world. The same weight will be judged significantly heavier if it was preceded by a lighter weight and will be judged lighter if preceded by one that is heavier. And in the realm of economic judgments and well-being, where ambiguity is even greater, the effects of comparison levels are even more striking. Studies looking at how happy or satisfied people are in different countries yield very surprising results. There is no greater report of happiness in

---

Addiction

Societies can display symptoms similar to a person's addictive-allergic reactions. An ideal example is the use of petroleum. Most of the overdeveloped countries in today's world have built their economy on a slippery foundation of oil, which is both dirty and dwindling. Car exhausts poison the air in major cities and expedite global warming. Spills from oil tankers damage miles of seashore, killing wildlife, ruining fisheries and rendering beaches unusable. At the same time, the world's reserves of petroleum are running out, and growing competition could become fierce in the coming decades.

Like an alcoholic or heroin addict, an overdeveloped country requires a steadily growing supply of its addictive substance (in this case petroleum) which imposes upon the system growing problems and weaknesses. Still, the weaker and sicker it becomes, the more of the substance it craves. And if the supply is threatened, the society can become desperate and irrational.

At the crux of planetary healing is the need to change the course of industrial development set by the western world, which has led to excessive consumption of the world's dwindling resources. It may not be necessary to sacrifice our life styles to cut back. Hopefully, we can learn to do more with less. Consider the bicycle, for example:

- Buying a car in a Third World country might cost five years' wages, while a bike may take five weeks to earn.
- 100 bikes can be made from the material in one average-sized car.
- In Great Britain it is estimated that if one-tenth of car trips under ten miles were made by bike, the nation would save upwards of 14 million barrels of oil a year. In the US, 40 percent of urban commuters drive less than four miles to work. Converting to bikes in these cases would clean up the air significantly.
- The bike is the most efficient form of human transport ever devised. A biker burns 35 calories per mile. A walker: 100 calories per mile. A bus using diesel fuel: 920 calories per mile per passenger. A car with one occupant: 1,860 calories per mile.

Japan than in many poor countries in Africa, no more in Western Europe than in Latin America. When one's whole country becomes wealthier one's frame of reference changes. One doesn't feel grateful one has more than people in poorer countries; one feels envious of those who are richer in one's own. The same studies that failed to show the expected differences between countries

---

* Traffic emissions help cause 30,000 deaths a year in the US.
* Pedaling keeps people healthy.

(The above facts and figures were borrowed from an article appearing in *WorldWatch Magazine*, July-August 1988, entitled "Pedaling into the Future," written by Marcia D. Lowe.)

A sensible step for societies today may be to combine all-weather bicycling (in canopied bicycle lanes) and electric cars (as soon as an effective battery or power source becomes available) for short trips. Mass transit systems—perhaps mag-lev buses and trains—could be used for long commutes.

Such a transportation system would help us get away from the automobile and our dangerous reliance on petroleum quickly, along with the filthy air, traffic congestion and gridlock they cause in most large cities. Imagine an elaborate network of bike paths drawn into the design of all urban and suburban areas, complete with safe parking and locker areas. People would be able to pedal safely to work or to a nearby mass transit station.

Such a transportation system is an ideal example of doing more with less. Another example is the electronics field where thousands of pages of information can now be stored on tiny chips and compact discs (CDs). Computer engineer Dean Kinard, a friend of mine, suggested to me the advantages of replacing today's voluminous metropolitan telephone books with CDs that contain not just local listings, but names and addresses of everyone in the country, or in the world for that matter. Telephones could be equipped with CD readers, autodialers, microcomputers, country code/area code libraries and an assortment of other features. Imagine the forests that will be saved when phone books are no longer printed. Next to go, perhaps: newspapers, magazines and books, all replaced by electronic reading devices.

Revolutionary means of transportation and communication that do more with less will require some major shifts in our ways of thinking and living, but the benefits that the changes will bring and the growing crises we'll inevitably face if we fail to change, say clearly that the time is now to vigorously promote them.

—MHM

did find that within each of them, those who were richer *were* more satisfied. *They* were comparing themselves to their neighbors, and that immediate comparison made a difference.

But clearly there is no real solution to our problems in that direction. Everyone can't be richer than everyone else. No matter how much an economy grows one thing can't be changed: Only 10% of the people can be in the 90th percentile. As a country's economy grows, and the incomes of everyone in it grow with it— or, more accurately, as the incomes of *many* grow; it seems not at all uncommon that there is also produced an underclass that shares scarcely at all in whatever fruits the growth does yield— people's frame of reference adjusts accordingly, and the overall contentment of the population rises little, and possibly even falls, as the frantic effort to grow takes its toll on other important aspects of human satisfaction (more on this shortly).

In the last 30 years, there has been *enormous* growth in the economy of the United States. Per capita Gross National Product (*after* correcting for inflation and taxes) is more than 150% of what it was when John Kennedy was inaugurated, and per capita *disposable* income (again inflation corrected) has risen even more. Moreover, if one looks at a variety of major consumer items that have contributed to our society's definition of the good life, one finds increases over the past three decades that are even more remarkable. The percentage of American homes with home freezers more than doubled; with clothes dryers more than *quadrupled*. The percentage of homes with air conditioning rose more than *five hundred percent* and with dishwashers more than *seven hundred percent*.

Yet over the same period of time, despite all that growth, reported levels of happiness in national surveys of subjective well-being have not surpassed the level reported in 1957, and for a number of years in that period they were significantly lower, despite the quite considerable overall economic growth in the interim. In 1958, John Kenneth Galbraith could aptly label us "The Affluent Society." By now, both "The Stuffed Society" and, ironically, "The Hungry Society" would be more fitting appellations.

A Societal Eating Disorder?

Thus still another analogy offers itself as a metaphor for our present condition: we seem to suffer from the societal equivalent of an eating disorder. We are trapped in a vicious circle of overconsumption of resources; severe social, personal, and environmental disruption; and then still further consumption as the purported cure for the very disorders overconsumption has brought about. The doctors for our social ills—primarily economists and the politicians who follow (and generate?) their theories—prescribe as the solution for all our social ills still greater economic growth, still more production and consumption. Indeed, we have reached a state of confusion of such proportions that we can regularly see on the pages of our leading newspapers and journals of opinion references to our "declining productivity" when what is really being referred to is a decline in the rate of *increase* in productivity. If we produce more per worker than the year before, but are not further *increasing* at the same rate, we seem to experience ourselves as declining.

The Social Neurosis of the Growth Society

Putting all these images together, still another, more comprehensive, analogy to individual illness suggests itself and may perhaps be the most useful in thinking about how to go about changing the patterns and circumstances that mock our seeming progress: We are suffering from what we might well label a social neurosis.

When individuals are neurotic, they engage repeatedly in behavior that is self-defeating and they construct defenses—often elaborate defenses—against recognizing the nature of their efforts and the reasons for their failure. Simple connections are not noticed or they are woven into a web of myths and distortions that keeps the individual from seeing clearly how his or her life is working and where and why it is working poorly. Often, the efforts the person makes in an effort to improve things turn out ironically to be perpetuating the very problem they are supposedly undertaken to solve. The person is caught in a vicious circle: The things he or she does to make things better make them worse, and the self-deceptions undertaken to protect him/her from the bitter truth keep the truth more bitter than it needs to be.

Thus, an individual who has grown up afraid of his angry, or even healthily assertive reactions to an extreme degree (perhaps because of parents who crushed his individuality and couldn't tolerate his growing assertiveness and power, or who were themselves too afraid of anger and disagreement to be able to accept it in their offspring) may engage in all sorts of efforts to prove to himself and to the world that he is in fact kind, nice, gentle, cooperative, etc. Because any even minimal signs of anger must be quashed and hidden, the slightest inclination in this direction leads to an excessive overreaction in the opposite direction. He is *excessively* nice, *excessively* cooperative, and as a consequence his own needs and feelings are poorly attended to. Unwittingly, other people, in the course simply of reacting to him, and to the distorted messages he gives out, play the role of ignoring or overriding his (insufficiently expressed) needs. And as a consequence, they are experienced (not necessarily consciously) as insensitive, mean, or selfish. Perceiving them this way, the neurotic is moved to anger; but anger, recall, is a forbidden emotion. So what does he do? What he always does: He attempts once again to quash the anger by being even more meek, kind, cooperative. And once again he sets the stage for his needs to be unmet and ignored, for still more anger to be generated, and for still further efforts to hide that anger by the same self-defeating behavior. Much of this goes on unconsciously, and the overall pattern—the repetitive, self-defeating nature of his way of life— consistently escapes him, even as it comes to dominate his daily experiences more and more. Thus does the ironic vicious circle of neurosis silently but inexorably stifle the individual's efforts to gain a reasonable measure of security and satisfaction in the world.

Let's look closely at the structural features of such a neurosis, rather than at the individual characteristics. The content of the concerns, obsessions, and self-defeating efforts that are made in any given case can vary from the excessive meekness described above, to excessive aggressiveness as a similarly self-defeating "cure" for feelings of insecurity, to patterns of withdrawal, of substance abuse, and so forth. It is in these *structural* features that we see an analogy to what is happening on a larger social scale.

If we observe the patterns of a growth society as a whole, we can see ironies and traps that seem to parallel closely the functioning of a neurotic individual. We see a society plagued by a growing sense of discontent, by a dangerous destructiveness toward the environment necessary to maintain it, by a fear of competition from competitors willing to live on less and therefore able to produce and sell more cheaply. And we see as well the continuing effort to try to "solve" these problems by somehow mobilizing still more growth and, as well, the continuing generation of myths that justify moving in this direction even as such movement exacerbates the very problems it is supposed to solve.

Myth I: Growth Will Make Us Content

Growth, we tell ourselves, is necessary to quell our discontents. Only if we make more, only if we *have* more, can we be content. The logic, at first, seems perfectly straightforward (as does the logic of any neurotic). What, unfortunately, makes neurosis so resistant to change is that the neurotic way of life seems to *make sense* to the neurotic. (Their *life* may not make sense to them; but subjectively it seems like everything except the premises of the neurosis is to blame.) If people are feeling discontent, feeling like they don't have enough, what could be more sensible (at least on a superficial level) than to attempt to quell such feelings by having more. If everyone had more, wouldn't we then all be content?

Well, as I indicated in the figures cited above for how much more we have now than when we were called "The Affluent Society," and how little that increase has produced contentment, the seeming logic of growth doesn't really square with the actual experiences of people living in the growth society. The reality is that we *have* grown and that it *hasn't* yielded the contentment that the growth myth says it should. Indeed, it *cannot*. For the very nature of a growth society is one in which central to it is the generation of desires. We have a multibillion dollar advertising industry to assure this, and this industry is only a part of the overall structure—social, economic, political, psychological—that maintains the continuing generation of new desires, the invidious experience of life that fuels the engines of growth but never quite brings us what we think we deserve.

So the pursuit of contentment through the expedient of growth ironically is one of the major sources of *discontent* in a society that is already affluent. Like the neurotic, we persist in the same direction, filling in the holes we have just dug for ourselves and—this is the essence of neurosis—seeing no other way as being possible.

Myth II: Growth Will Eliminate Poverty

In a similar vein, we attempt via growth to solve the problems of poverty that persist despite our society's overall enormous wealth. Once again we tell ourselves that growth is the answer when it is really a good part of the problem. If only we can grow, if only we had more, we say, then there would be enough to go around and poverty would be ended.

Again the logic is at first seductively appealing. But it ignores the overall imperatives, the overall way of life of the growth society. It ignores in particular two key characteristics of a society such as ours. First of all, much of our poverty has a comparative element. In the sad and beautiful film "El Norte," about the plight of two Guatemalan peasants who attempt to escape oppression and live a better life in the United States, Rosa and Enrique are awed by the flush toilet and the refrigerator in the first apartment they are shown in the golden land of California. The affluent North American viewer is more apt to be shocked by the squalor and the filth of the same apartment. So too, after a period of exposure to the very different standards of an affluent society, are the Rosas and Enriques who continue to flock to North America and to Western Europe in search of the good life. It is not long before such apartments are transformed in their experience from symbols of affluence to symbols of poverty. For the "growth fix" solution ignores the fact that it hurts to be low man on the totem pole no matter how high the pole.

Rosa and Enrique's experiences illustrate both and the failure of the growth approach to poverty. It is certainly true that the idea of growth would not have such a hold on us if it did not produce *some* benefits—indeed, benefits more readily observable and more immediately experienced than the more delayed, and more complex, contradictions. Millions of people would not flock to the developed countries if they were not spurred by the misery in their own lands or by the apparent appeal of life in "El Norte." Though flush toilets and refrigerators are not an unmixed blessing from an ecological perspective, few of us who have experienced their conveniences would be willing to do without them or hesitant to say that, in terms of ease of living, they are a quite considerable improvement. Growth does in that sense improve the human lot.

But if the poor in America, who almost always have not only flush toilets and refrigerators but radios and television sets as well or at least who do *if* they are not homeless, as increasing numbers in the growth-oriented societies are, for reasons not so extrinsic to the impulsions of growth—they may perhaps be forgiven for not being as enthusiastic about the grimy slums in which these toilets and refrigerators are found as were, for a brief time, Rosa and Enrique. Yes, our poor are in some ways rich by world standards. Growth has brought them things. But living in a society whose standards and expectations rise in tandem with material growth, a society which apportions very unequally not only income but education, health care, and the possibility for work that brings self respect, they indeed live the lives of poor people.

If we look beneath the surface, we can see that the strategy of ending the poverty in affluent societies via the expedient of growth is really a way of avoiding the true source of poverty in those societies, which is inequality. As standards rise for the majority in the population, so—appropriately and understand-ably—do the expectations of those at the bottom. And when they are locked out of the way of life available to most people in the society, it is that fact, and not the fact that they have "more" than their equivalents did years before that defines their experience of themselves. Ultimately, however disguised it may sometimes be, the growth strategy is essentially a version of the "trickle-down" approach, in which accumulation of still more by the haves is supposed to yield beneficial side effects for the have-nots. What results, however, is that the poor wind up with the same small proportion of the new larger total product that they had of the earlier. It is simply inequality at a higher level.

"A rising tide lifts all boats," said John F. Kennedy in a clever, but terribly misleading, phrase. Well, the tide *has* risen. As the figures I cited earlier show clearly, there has been enormous growth in our economy in the last 30 years. But anyone with even minimal powers of observation or empathy can see that, notwithstanding that growth, the neighborhoods of the poor today are at least as sad and frightening as they were then. For the people living in our inner cities, all the rising tide has done is to make it harder for them to keep their heads above water.

Myth II (Continued): Growth Will Heighten Generosity Toward Those in Need

We have seen that the attempt to eliminate poverty through growth is frustrated by the continually rising expectations of a growth society, which yield continuing misery for those with the smallest pieces even as the size of the pie keeps increasing; it falters as well on the repeatedly frustrated assumption that with an increasing standard of living the comfortable majority will be more willing to devote a portion of *their* increasing wealth to those more in need. The 1980s have been a decade of almost continuous growth of the American economy (only in 1982 did the real GNP not increase). Yet they have also been a time when the War on Poverty was rather thoroughly replaced by a War on Taxes, a war whose greatest casualties were those who desperately needed the social programs that we somehow could not now "afford," though we could afford them readily when the overall size of the economy was much smaller. We tell ourselves that we will better be able to help the poor when we all are richer, but we keep finding that we are not yet rich enough and that still more always seems to be required.

In a growth economy desires rise continually. (As I noted earlier, for the economy to grow desires *must* keep increasing.) Therefore, despite the increasing wealth of the populace, there is no guarantee whatsoever that generosity will grow with the economy. The forces of greed and individualistic striving, released so fully in the 1980s and justified in the name of promoting growth, were devastating to those in need. Far from benefitting the poor, our way of organizing our lives around more and more goods cast their needs into last place. Once again, the myths of the growth economy served the same function as the self-deceptions of the neurotic: providing a rationale for continuing along a path that doesn't work and a smokescreen to blunt perception of both the damage and its connection to the choices we make—indeed, perception of the very fact that we *are* making choices, that there are alternatives that we have failed to recognize or consider.

Myth III: Growth Will Provide
the Resources to Clean Up the Environment

Finally, the social neurosis of growth, with its ironies and unnecessary self-defeats shows itself perhaps most strikingly in our relation to the life-sustaining environment. Via thinking that is reminiscent of the denial that helps maintain many individual neuroses, we keep expecting that somehow a technological fix will make our environmental problems go away. And, in the view of some economists, it is indeed only growth that can provide us with the capital to finance that fix. Some come close to averring that pollution is itself a good, since cleaning it up is another potential growth industry. It is of course possible that a technological fix can be found. Indeed, despite the caricature frequently offered of those who oppose our society's dominant religion of growth, I myself am very much in favor of promoting research to find cleaner sources of energy and even to find ways of increasing productivity if it can be done in an environmentally benign way.

But that is a far cry from simply saying let's try to grow in every way possible and assume that "somehow" all that accumulated capital will automatically solve our problems. Random, helter-skelter behavior, especially random helter-skelter behavior of the very sort that has *created* our problems—simply trying to produce more and more of whatever we possibly can—seems to me highly unlikely to yield a solution to our environmental crisis. It has been the forces (and the proponents) of growth that have *blocked* research and development in such areas as solar energy, as they have blocked efforts at conservation. There is money to be made in what can be *sold* most readily and most profitably, and that is far from synonymous with the technology that we need in order to repair the damage we have done and continue to do.

My prime nominee for a social pattern that replicates individual neurosis is the effort to solve the deterioration of the environment through still more growth. If ever we engage on a societal level in the very behavior that is causing the trouble, in the blind hope that it will be the solution instead, here it is. Now of course, any neurosis that is maintained for a while must have a decent cover, a rationale that its practitioner can believe, and that is true here as well; there certainly is a need for more research on alternative technologies and on means to clean up the mess that already exists. But to question the imperative of growth, to question a way of life in which growth is the *aim* rather than the sometime product of efforts that are focused more directly on addressing real human needs, is not to foreclose the future. Indeed, it is to try to assure one.

The Ironies and Contradictions of the Growth Imperative

As with the neuroses of individuals, the societal patterns that I have nominated as at least first cousins of neurosis are perhaps saddest of all in the fact that they are so unnecessary, that they result from misperceptions and miscalculations about what is truly gratifying. It would be one thing if we were risking our health and our futures in the pursuit of genuine pleasures. That might be short-sighted or foolish, but it would not be quite the waste that our present patterns are. For as the figures cited above indicate, growth has not brought us the happiness we expected. Indeed, in important ways its pursuit has been a source of pain and frustration.

In the effort to produce more, to increase "efficiency" and "productivity," we have undermined some of the things that play a more significant role in feeling contented and secure than do the goods around which our lives are organized. One out of five Americans, for example, moves each year, many in the pursuit of a "better" (usually this means simply higher paying) job or a bigger (and hence "better") home. What does this do to the sense of community? To the stability of friendships? To family?

In America it is now the exception to find a family in which children, parents, and grandchildren all live in the same city, or even in the same state. The security that comes with having people around one who can automatically be counted on, like the security that comes with being a part of a community that has known one all one's life and has a more or less automatic "place" for one, has largely vanished for most Americans. And to compensate for this, many unwittingly turn instead to "success" to quell the gnawing sense of contingency that is the human condition. But when one's income, one's possessions, the size of one's house, become the guarantors of one's feeling OK in the world, this begins to feed on itself. For as one gears up to increase one's income—perhaps by working longer hours; or moving to find a better opportunity; or working under a degree of pressure that takes its toll when we come home, on relations with our spouse, on the time and energy to see friends, on how one is with one's children—one undermines further the other foundations of a sense of well-being and thus feels still more dependent on the material and economic side of life to compensate. And of course the predictable result is that still further distortions occur, and the need for "more" recreates itself once again out of the ashes of community and relatedness.

Is There a Cure?: Economic Growth and Personal Growth

In a general way it may be said that the direction for a healing change lies in reorienting our society from an emphasis on economic growth to one on personal growth; attending less to what we have and more to who we are and to the true sources of contentment and satisfaction. Such a change would lead us away from patterns of increasing consumption of natural resources and the creation of endless needs and desires. It would enable us to develop our capacities for self-awareness, for creative leisure, and for deep and enduring relationships.

But a shift from economic to psychological growth is not without its problems. A prominent line of recent social criticism has complained that ours is *too* psychologically oriented a society, that we have created an age of "Psychological Man," a "culture of narcissism." There is much that is useful in these critiques if they are placed in the proper context, but they are also potentially very misleading. Far from being a culture that is too psychologically oriented we are much more accurately described as psychologically impoverished. We remain in the era of Economic Man, dominated not primarily by the quest for a truer expression of our deepest nature or more gratifying and mutually supportive relationships to others, but by the quest for more money and goods, for "making it." Especially is this so in our collective behavior as a society. As individuals, there is evidence that we are beginning to see the limitations of this way of life and to seek after goals more truly related to well-being. But our actions as a society—the people we elect, the legislation we pass (and don't pass), the way we set up the world of work and orient to it—get in the way of these individual efforts.

Those who see the rise of Psychological Man are observing the individual efforts at self-healing that are made necessary in large measure by what we continue to do to ourselves as members of a society dedicated to the promotion of Economic Man. (The use of the masculine generic here is not accidental. It is both the terminology on which these battles have been fought thus far and a reflection of the gender relations that have been common as we have organized our lives around production values instead of experiential values.) At the margins of the society, in the realm of private life, can be seen the stirrings of efforts to live in the way that the affluence we have achieved should permit us. The growth we have achieved was not all founded on error. Our technological society, in principle, can remove from our lives the drudgery and scraping for subsistence that have been the lot of many of our forebears. But we have failed really to appreciate what we have achieved, and in so failing have diminished it. Rather than exploring the possibilities for leisure and self-development our affluence has afforded us, we continue to pursue greater and greater product as if we were still poor, and in the process we make ourselves *feel* poor.

It is true that many of the psychologically oriented efforts to transcend the limits of the way of life we have created have ended up replicating that way of life. In that sense, the critics of Psychological Man have been correct. Much of what has arisen from the human potential movement has been not only shallow but self-defeating. But it has been so not because it was too psychologically oriented but because it was oriented around the wrong psychology—indeed around a psychology that was itself a reflection of the actual dominance in our lives of the structures of mind and habits of thought of Economic Man. As Barry Schwartz has shown in his interesting and important book, *The Battle for Human Nature*, much of our psychological theorizing is built upon the same individualistic values, the same assumptions of "natural" competitiveness and selfishness on which our economic system is founded. Such a psychology, which unwittingly piggybacks on the very assumptions we need to transcend, cannot take us very far in the effort to build a new way of life.

But this narrowly self-oriented approach, unappreciative of context or interdependency, enamored with a kind of self-development and self-expression that puts the needs of others at a remove, is but a caricature of how a psychology truly oriented to human potential and human values would look. It is the secret stepchild of Economic Man and its unwitting allegiance to the latter constrains its possibilities for liberation.

Is There a Cure?: Concrete Changes and Political Action

Some of the concrete changes I believe are needed to heal us and relieve our dangerous contradictions are spelled out in *The Poverty of Affluence*. They include job-sharing as a means of dealing with unemployment rather than "creating" jobs (which necessarily means also creating new products and creating new needs for them); new means and patterns of transportation that are at once more energy-efficient, more healthful, and more pleasant; taking much of the fruits of our productive capacities in leisure rather than in goods; focusing our efforts on developing the arts, recreational facilities, and education; and reexamining our relation to our communities and to each other.

None of these changes are likely to be effective or enduring without also attending very focally to the political. I cannot spell out in a brief chapter either all the changes needed or all the obstacles that exist. Nor, of course, is the limitation simply one of space. I do not *know* all that has to be done. I can offer only the bare outlines that thus far seem discernible. But one thing seems to me particularly clear. If we separate the psychological and the political—if we attempt to achieve a kind of mass therapy of society without seeing the need for an enormous amount of political organizing; or if we, conversely, devote ourselves to a politics that, like so many political movements of the past, is insufficiently attentive to the experiences of individual human beings—we will fail.

Our craving for possessions is an effort to compensate for something deep and basic that is missing from our lives. Our technological achievements have the potential to make our lives freer of anxiety and drudgery than any society in history. The possibilities open to us are truly extraordinary. But first we must recognize the enormous distortions and dangers that have also entered our lives in the industrial era. Perhaps in some sense those distortions were once necessary. Perhaps without them we never could have gotten to the point we are now, with the possibility of longer, healthier, more fulfilling lives than any population has ever experienced. But we will not realize that possibility if we continue on our present course. If we continue to strive after more and more goods, if we continue to define our lives by narrow "bottom line" considerations, we will instead further tighten the vicious circle I have described. And in the process not only will we fail to enjoy the fruits of our progress, we may also damage severely the ecosystem that sustains our very lives. It is time for us to recognize our affluence before we destroy both it and ourselves. If we keep wanting more, the continually expanding—and fragile—bubble of our civilization will burst. If we instead seek to create a new balance, to direct our attention and our efforts to community, to concrete human experience, to our relations with each other, we may yet cure ourselves.

In the treatment of any neurosis insight is essential, but it is never enough. Action too is required to change the conditions that recreate the neurotic way of life over and over again. The path to cure is always difficult, and it is inevitably marked by frustrating loops and snares that seem to lead us back to the thickets from which we seek escape. But change is aided by the converse of the forces that sustain our persistence in self-defeat. If we begin to take steps to change, that change can feed on itself. For right steps have consequences just as wrong ones do. Each step we take off the treadmill of materialism weakens its hold on us, as it builds the alternative that heretofore we have consistently undermined.

It is extremely difficult for us to extricate ourselves individually from the patterns I have described here. Indeed, the seeking after individual solutions is part of the very denial of a shared fate that is at the heart of our problem. But if we can find a way jointly to mobilize for change, we can gain some strength from the knowledge that as hard as it is to take the first steps in overcoming a neurotic way of life, each step taken makes the next just a bit easier.

Chapter Seven:
Swadhyaya:
The Silent, Singing Revolution of India

by Majid Rahnema

His background. Retired ambassador for Iran and a grassroots learner/philosopher. Many articles, lectures and seminars on societal, transcultural and international issues, focusing on the impacts of modernization and economization of life on indigenous societies. Visiting professor to many universities in Europe and North America. Educational and development consultant to countries in Africa and Asia. Has held several UN positions. Fluent in Persian, English and French. Passable Russian, Arabic and Spanish. Doctorate in Law, Sorbonne.

His chapter. In recent years the Swadhyaya movement in India has burgeoned from nine members to several million, all devoted to self-realization and divine brotherhood. Swadhyaya communities are driven by the pursuit of wholesomeness rather than economic betterment. Compared to other communities, they are indeed more wholesome ... but also better developed economically, cleaner, and more efficient. The people are enthusiastic and mutually respectful.

One cannot help but rejoice that there are a growing number of people using their divine intelligence and imagination.

7. Swadhyaya:
The Silent, Singing Revolution of India

by Majid Rahnema

Of all the lands where interesting events are happening at the grassroots, India seems to provide the curious explorer with an endless journey into serendipity. One goes to discover a particular thing, only to find a half-open door which unexpectedly invites one to take a totally different direction.

I went to India in 1988 to find out what had happened to *Nai Taleem*, the "Basic Education Scheme" which had been proposed by Mahatma Gandhi in 1937, and almost immediately after, tried out in some nine Indian states. I was somewhat disappointed to realize that the imported "modern" school system had "phagocytized" the original schools, so beautifully conceived by Gandhi. Some two hundred of them are still functioning against wind and tide. As a rule, however, the Gandhian dream has been reduced and transformed into an Indian and rural version of the Montessori schools. It was during a visit to these centres around Vedchi, in the Surat region near Bombay, that I was informed about a new movement, the Swadhyaya, which was now quite active in hundreds of villages in Maharashtra and Gujarat.

Back in Delhi, friends and colleagues of mine at the Centre for the Study of Developing Societies confirmed the fact. Two of them who were researching the movement[1] mentioned that, although the Swadhyaya came into being in the 1950s, very few people even in Delhi had heard about it. The Centre itself had come to know of its existence only by the end of 1986 when it had received an invitation to attend a huge gathering in Allahabad to which had come some 400,000 Swadhyayees from all over India. The friend who had attended the meeting on behalf of the Centre told me that the problem with studying Swadhyaya as a social scientist is that you quickly lose your objectivity, for you cannot observe lifestyles in remote villages in India without relating. And then there goes your "academic distance."

To get a closer view of this phenomenal movement, I made two visits to India, in 1988 and early 89. These visits allowed me to make a number of trips to Swadhyayee villages in Gujarat, Maharashtra and Daman. There, I had long talks and interviews with the persons directly involved in Swadhyaya and with other informed persons. More particularly, I had the unique privilege of meeting many times *Dadaji*, the man who inspired the whole movement and who still remains its leading heart and mind. I accompanied Dadaji for some ten days on his pilgrimages to faraway villages.

The Modern Man of Action in the Vedic Tradition

The soul behind the Swadhyaya is a great and playful master of words, a remarkable representative of one of the oldest and richest oral civilizations of the world, a born teacher, and a modern man of action in the Vedic traditions of India. His real name is Pandurang Shastri Aijnath Athavale. But he is affectionately referred to, by the millions who know him, as Dadaji, *dada* meaning elder brother. Dadaji is now over 68, although he appears much younger. He is a scholar in Sanskrit and Hindu classics, though in his talks he abundantly refers to such vast an array of Western and other philosophers as Marx, Nietzche, Freud, Bertrand Russell, Gabriel Marcel and Sartre, amongst others, whom he has read in English. All this, without having ever regularly attended school, or received any diploma. His father, a well known master of Sanskrit, had set up in Bombay some fifty years ago a *Pathshala* (a seat of nonformal learning in Vedic thought) where he was teaching and preaching. Dada, at the age of 34, continued the tradition after his father's death.

For Dada, the Sunday's preachings at the Pathshala were only the first steps in realizing his dream of responding in an Indian yet creative fashion, to the sufferings of the millions. He was convinced that if the ordinary people would only be informed of the Gita teaching, that would help them find the most relevant answers to their problems. Swadhyaya was imagined by him as the "stream" called to help him achieve this task.

Discovering the Divine Within Oneself

Although it is almost impossible to translate the word in any language, the sanskrit term *swadhyaya* means literally in sanskrit, study, knowledge or discovery (*adhyaya*) of the self (*swa*). It seems that, for Dada, such a study should aim at knowing both the self in its Vedic sense, and the ego, which is one's own made up and distorted image of the self. Dada recognizes that the ego, or the "I" feeling, is an obstacle to "enlightened self-development." But

---

Overcoming Addiction

Addiction is any relationship to a substance, a person or an activity that makes people's lives continually worse, yet they continue regardless. It is often the result of emotional wounds received during childhood. When children's deep-seated needs for love or acceptance or appreciation are not met, they tend to bring secrecy and mistrust along with them into adulthood. Until they heal those early wounds, as through therapy, they will never be able to enjoy happy, trusting relationships with others. They remain uneasy in friendships and at work. They remain trapped in the vicious circle of their addiction, thinking that their behavior will improve their mood when actually, except for the initial, short-lived highs, their mood grows continually darker.

When we support and assist family members or close friends trapped in on-going struggles with drugs, eating disorders, alcoholism, workaholism, sexual misconduct, gambling, compulsive shopping, or another form of addiction, we are assuming they will eventually free themselves from their problem. If they fail to do so, our continued support eventually begins to enable their addiction and self-destructive tendencies. We begin to make the problem worse. What they really need is assistance by caring, experienced individuals in satisfying deep-seated needs that were never met in childhood.

Entire societies can display addictive behavior, as shown in the preceding chapter. Is today's overdeveloped civilization the result of a perpetual quest to satisfy unmet needs? Is our unquenchable desire for more merchandise and bigger homes caused by something basic and vital, something warm and human that is missing from our lives?

Apparently so. We in the West seem to be short on the sense of community and familial love that keep societies stable.

Movements are underway in many countries to regain a sense of community. In the US there are community-building workshops by such love-fueled thinkers as M. Scott Peck. In India there is the Swadhyaya movement, the subject of Chapter 7.

—MHM

he assumes that if it is recognized as such, it can pave the way to the ultimate discovery of the Atman, the "selfless" self which makes the latter a part and parcel of the cosmic self, and the manifestation of the God within each individual. The ego should therefore "be treated like a shirt which can be removed from the body as and when desired," says Dada.

Swadhyaya is based on the assumption that the twin principle of the Vedantas, *Tat-Twam-Asi* (You are Him, or Thou art that) and *Aham-Brahma-Asmi* (I am divine), constitute an eternal truth. In other words, our deeper, cosmic Self is inhabited by the *Yogeshwar* or God. The understanding of this Truth, that God is both within and with us, enables us to realize that "God does not work for you from a distant place or remote heaven. He is with you and works with you provided you do your utmost."[2] This "divine presence" within helps us to realize the "we-feeling," and the fact that "to be is to be related."

Relating to Each Other in Knowledge, Devotion and Action

For Dada, three old Vedic paths, *Jnana*, *Bhakti* and *Karma*, remain as valid as when they were first discovered. Fully understood, in their spirit, and "joined together," they can help human beings change their world of violence and conflicts and put an end to their miseries.

Jnana is knowledge, starting indeed with self-knowledge. The latter means more than introspection. It means meeting others to know our Self. Through knowledge, one realizes that "love of God within implies love and affection towards His Universe. This love or reverence for our fellow-beings is bound to be translated into altruistic actions. . . . It is bound to result in selfless activism."[2]

Bhakti means devotion. For Dada, this devotion to the Source, to the God within one, is the essence of religion, a concept which religionists have totally distorted and transformed into a hodge-podge of sacerdotalism, of rituals and negativism. True religion, or Dharma,[3] is the opposite of sacerdotalism. It is a philosophy of life which "teaches us to develop respect and reverence for the whole of creation." It reflects the awareness that my body, like any one's else, is "a dwelling place" of the Creator, whether one calls it God, Allah, Yogeshwar, Krishna or Shiva.

Awareness of this truth will make one respect oneself as
well as others. This gives firm basis and, I am sure, the
right basis to socialism or democratic socialism. It gives
dignity to every human being. God is within me. He is the
operator of my body. But why should He operate my
body? Because He needs me. I therefore ought to respond
to this trust.[2]

Bhakti represents one's response to this "trust." It is an accepted
Vedic practice that two days in a month (11th day of each half of
the lunar month), are pious days to be devoted to prayers and
actions in the service of God. For Dada, the Yogeshwar in us does
not need the ritualistic forms of Bhakti or devotion preached by
religionists. He needs us whenever and wherever we can help
him reach other human beings who have not yet fully realized the
divine presence within them. So, he suggests, the two days could
more usefully express our devotion if spent to pay someone a
devotional visit or a *bhaktiferi*, the intention being to help that
person to realize his or her divine, yet untapped, capacities.

The last of the three paths is Karma or "selfless action." In the
Hindu scripture of the Geeta, says Dada, Krishna teaches doing
one's duty without attachment to the result. Thus, the Yogeshwar
within everyone operates in a *Leela* or "Divine sport" fashion. In
this traditional context:

God is a "Cosmic Player" and his creative activity has no
other extraneous or ulterior motive; it is without any
practical consideration of loss or gain. We are not mere
helpless creatures or puppets in the hands of the
supernatural being. We are participants in God's Divine
and creative play. Let us, therefore, understand the game,
and play it sincerely and knowingly as well as
spontaneously and joyfully.[2]

How the Nineteen Became the Millions

The Swadhyaya *parivar* (the Hindi word for family) which is
now over three million, started with a pilgrimage of the 19 earlier
attendants of Dada's Sunday's talks at the Pathshala. Long
personal dialogues and walks on the Bombay beach brought
Dadaji to undertake, one day, what he thought was the "right
action": to use bhaktiferi (devotional visits) as a means of
regenerating the "divine" relationships called to tie together the
human family.

To start the movement, Dada asked the 19 to form small groups of 4 to 5 persons and go for a couple of weeks to a number of villages in Gujarat just to talk to people as brothers meeting for the first time. Many of these earlier pilgrims were quite rich people accustomed to an easy life. Yet Dada had urged them to live during these bhaktiferis exactly like the villagers they were going to meet, never asking anyone for food or shelter. They were also asked never to give anyone lectures or "recipes" for a better life. Their only task was to show them that the affection and respect they were bringing was a gift of the God within them.

"We followed rather reluctantly what he had asked us to do," one of the first pilgrims confessed to me. "We did it only because we had faith in him, but deep in our minds we had serious doubts that such tours would ever work. . . . The first years were particularly deceptive, for we had the impression that nothing was happening. Our presence continued to be interpreted with suspicion. The residents wondered if we were planning to buy them out for electoral purposes. Were we seeking to indoctrinate them to some new cult? It was anyhow clear to the local people that no outsider, in particular well-off and educated persons from the cities, would come only to greet them without any ulterior motive. It took them years to realize that we actually had no other motive but to relate to them as brothers, and through the same God inhabiting us all. But when they did, the impossible had happened. We started to relate to each other as divine brothers."

The original group of 19 had to go back to the same villages for 8 to 10 years, for almost two weeks every year. In the meantime, others had started similar devotional visits. In the beginning, even when the local populations had ultimately come to believe in the sincerity of the new pilgrims, their attitudes toward them were still ambiguous. In many cases, they preferred to ask their new, educated brothers for assistance, rather than taking any initiative of their own. For Dada, however, it was out of the question that any supportive action from "headquarters" would come without the local populations having taken the initiative for it.

Thus, for some 20 years, the nascent small groups of Swadhyayee travelled from all directions to the many pilgrimage centres of India, visiting unknown, divine brothers. New people were now joining them in growing numbers. The pilgrimages were usually ending up with tirthayatras (travelling to and gathering at the pilgrim centres), often in Dada's presence. From 1981 to 1985, some 25 meetings of the sort had taken place, now involving hundreds of thousands of individuals.

The first all-India gathering (*milan*), which crowned these activities, was the *Tirthraj milan* which, in the Spring of 1986, brought together more than 300,000 Swadhyayees. The gathering was held in Prayag (Allahabad), where the three holy rivers, the Ganga, the Yamuna and the invisible Saraswati, meet. A virtually new city was built in a month by as many as 15,000 volunteers who worked in rotation for a whole month, rapidly installing tents and other accommodations and facilities to provide hospitality for some 500,000 people. No outside money was spent for the whole operation, including the township, which was built up and dismantled in an unbelievably short time. Only 4 million Rupees worth of suitable cloth had been brought from the mills for the construction of residential tents. Yet even this sum was "recycled" at the end of the meeting as the Swadhyayees proposed to Dada to buy at least 2.5 meters cloth each. This material is now used, in most Swadhyayee families, either as bedcovers, or wrapped separately as a most cherished souvenir.[4]

The Tirthraj gathering is only one example of the extraordinary vitality of the Swadhyaya movement, or stream, as Dada likes to call it. It seems that, after a long period of "underground" formation, the many little springs and brooks which had started to run, as a result of the early bhaktiferies, joined each other, at a later stage, to form a huge river of unexpected proportions, similar to the rivers meeting at Prayag.

A Different Perception of Reality

The facts confronting the Swadhyayees are in many ways similar to those confronted by the millions of people generally classified as "have-nots," "under-developed," "helpless," "poor" or "oppressed" of the world. What makes the first major difference is that the Swadhyayees have come to share a new perception of the same facts.

This new perception is built on the vision, common to almost all the world's societies, that sufferings and miseries are facts of life, the heaviest burdens always falling on the shoulders of those living at the bottom of various societal pyramids. For the

Swadhyayee, this vision is coupled, however, with the belief that there is a God within one's immediate reach who can make it possible to put an end to those sufferings. Yet, these remain only the symptoms of a much more momentous phenomenon: the alienation of Man from his divine essence.[5] To bring technological or fragmented solutions to particular pains of an immediate nature might only alleviate or reduce a number of symptoms. It never eliminates their fundamental causes. More, to reduce the scope of one's action into fighting a number of self-picked "enemies" or "outer causes" is another way of avoiding the real issues. This also tends to dissipate one's vital energy which should always be directed toward the essential.

Serious, long-lasting, revolutionary changes are only possible if one rediscovers, honors, listens to, and follows the divine Source within one. The God-like power gained by this very awareness not only provides one with all the means and resources necessary to confront reality, but also eventually to change that reality. The same awareness prevents a Swadhyayee from being impressed by manipulative "saviours" who come to him with ready-made solutions and offers of financial or technical assistance. The Swadhyayee no longer perceives himself as helpless, weak or called to be assisted or "saved." With the God within him, he feels that he is, in fact, much less dependent on needs, compared to the "powerful" whose insatiable needs can never be satisfied.

This change of perception is no doubt due primarily to Dada's personality, his sensitivity to people's feelings, his great knowledge of the Indians' cultural heritage and, indeed, his charismatic and truly convivial relationship with every other member of the Swadhyaya parivar. Whenever Dada addresses a group, whatever its size, one has the feeling that he takes them on a guided tour into their own inner temple, enchanting them with his colourful presentations of the Yogeshwar inhabiting them, and introducing them to all the marvelous things He can do for everyone. These guided inner tours are always a festivity and a cathartic "happening" for all. During each of these happenings, the charismatic vibrations sent by this magician of orality seem to carry his listeners to peaceful and beautiful heights, giving them a feeling of oneness with everything. Dada talks to them about the oldest Gods, Goddesses and heroes of yester-years, as if they were still alive and active in their midst. For awhile, myths become realities and realities are perceived in their transcendental truth. All his utterings, including his significant moments of silence, are so charged with compassion that people do feel divine, as they listen to him. They are deeply touched that they are respected or treated equally not for charitable reasons, but because of their own divine qualities. Moreover, it is God who needs *them*. With Dada and the other members of the parivar, they feel proud to respond to that need.

Dada's talks are always down to earth, however. His words and stories are easy to understand. He makes people laugh at simple things, although he regards the laughter as a reminder to everyone that to host a God on a permanent basis is not an easy task. Yet, as he is fully conscious of everyone's weaknesses, he is particularly careful not to give a guilty conscience to anyone. Although he is a convinced vegetarian, whenever he is in the homes of fishing communities he shows great respect for their eating habits. In that, contrary to Gandhi, he avoids imposing austerity and ascetic behaviour on people who are not yet ready for it.[6]

To sum up, it could be said that Swadhyayees, as a whole, have now gained a new perception of their reality. It is a perception quite different from that prevailing around them, particularly amongst those totally colonized by the ideals of *homo economicus* and his consumer society. The worldview they share has enabled them to live their life with greater ease and grace, while it has regenerated their bonds with the essence of their cultural heritage. Altogether, it has made them more aware of both their potentialities and limitations. More than anything else, they now know the nature of their own forms of power. Having gained a more holistic view of their reality, they are certainly less lured by outside promises of assistance and no longer harbour wild illusions of "solutions" of a fragmented or superficial nature.

Different Incentives

A major consequence of this different perception of reality has been a corresponding change in the Swadhyayee's basic incentives in life. To anyone visiting a Swadhyayee community, it appears almost immediately that economic incentives are much weaker here compared to other communities, particularly in urban areas. In fact, one of the most thought-provoking contributions of Swadhyaya to alternative approaches to development is that it has re-embedded economy (to paraphrase Polanyi's expression) in its wider societal context, as it had always been. The modern economic paradigm falls apart as more powerful incentives, such as self-realization, now govern all social activities, including the production of resources.

What is most extraordinary and somewhat paradoxical is that the *spiritual* overtones in the incentives inspiring the ordinary Swadhyayee, have led to a much greater *economic* prosperity of the Swadhyayee villages. An amazing illustration of this fact may be seen in the numerous Bhakti-based orchards and farms created by the members of the parivar. As a rule, the economic prosperity and productivity of these nonprofit farms are often incomparably better than the individual profit-based farms surrounding them. When the outsider asks a Swadhyayee the reasons for the difference, the answer is inevitably: "Well, here God has done the work through his children, whereas the others are only the work of ordinary human beings working for themselves!!"

The Parivar Spirit

The parivar spirit could be described by a combination of the following principles and practices, most of which are particular to the Swadhyaya movement.

1. As one realizes the divine qualities within oneself and learns to relate with others, not only are one's own potentialities for taking the right action maximised, but the same multiplying effect is produced at the level of the entire group. As the Swadhyayee is not only part of one's own inherited family but also of the entire Swadhyaya parivar, all members of that extended family each have the feeling that their own part in improving their life has been performed to the best of their ability.

2. The same processes of self-realization and self-knowledge lead to a deeper understanding of the roots (and the sap) which are instrumental in the preservation and the strengthening of one's extended cultural family. Hence, one's glorious heritage[7] should be studied in a creative and responsible manner. Such a study would show that the teaching of the old seers reflected a timeless truth, the full understanding of which is a *sine qua non* condition for its adaptation to modern conditions.[8]

3. Social action and the regeneration of people's living space are thus, fundamentally, a problem of attending the roots and keeping them alive and in good shape. This constant attention to the roots leads one to focusing on the essential, rather than dissipating one's energy on meaningless and secondary issues.

For example, Dada does not believe in the wisdom of mobilizing people's energy to fight the caste system on legal or formal grounds, or simply because that seems to represent outdated and undemocratic practices. The caste system, he believes, is part of a holistic worldview of many complex dimensions. To translate it into a modern concept of fictitious equality and thus to reduce it to a political issue of fashionable or demagogic nature, is to hinder rather than to foster the processes required for the elimination of dehumanizing and exploitative social barriers.

The question should therefore be re-examined thoroughly and in a holistic fashion, in particular in the light of the traditions underlying it. This would anyhow help one understand that such deeply rooted beliefs and practices can never be wiped out, only as a result of illusory and fragmented reactions to some of their syndromes.

4. The question of power (and of empowerment, its corollary), an issue of particular concern to most grassroots movements, is perceived here in the same context. For the very notion of *Aham-Brahma-Asmi* excludes, by definition, the concept of anyone's powerlessness. The belief that every individual has potentially the power of a God, only makes it important that this power be discovered and used in a righteous fashion.

In practical terms again, this means that each Swadhyayee should be fearless in defending truth, as Valmiki, the author of *Ramayan* was when "he could not bear the strong and the powerful exploiting the weak and the oppressed for their pleasure and pastime."[8]

This does not mean at all to become involved in power politics. In actuality, Dada makes sure that the movement is kept out of conventional party or power politics. Members of the parivar may join any political organization of their choice, yet Dada categorically refuses that the movement be used by anyone for political purposes. Neither does he try to seize power or political positions, anywhere. Instead, members of the parivar seem to have already filtered into many an important administration and organization as welcome, responsible members.

Their network is operating like a new freemasonry at the service of the grassroots populations. In a Swadhyayee village, no outsider would ever try to run for any public office if the parivar has already agreed to present its own member for that office.

5. In the parivar spirit, self-reliance is not only a moral attitude, but a direct consequence of the power derived from the constant interaction with the inner divine source. The assumption remains that if God's presence within any single individual makes him or her free from any dependence on others, the same applies to the whole group. As such, Dada has systematically and categorically refused any assistance from outside. Even when the wealthy members of the parivar seek to make important contributions to the collective funds, they need to wait long before Dada accepts them. One such donor told me that he had to wait four years before Dada was convinced that the gesture represented a genuine, selfless *Bhakti* toward God, rather than a contribution to the movement.

6. Finally, the total absence of conventional organizational structures is another very distinctive expression of the parivar spirit. As already referred to, Swadhyaya has no administrative setup, no status, no president or secretary general, no board of directors, no organizational chart, not even any registered member. To this date, it has functioned like a real family, even though its size has grown to over three million members. Dada is both its elder brother and father. His daughter *Didi* (younger sister), a young lady with an extremely warm and convivial presence, is already emerging as the unanimously accepted heiress in line. At the district level, an informal group of activists or respected notables coordinate various activities in their areas, and are in constant touch with the Bombay Headquarters. They are called *motabhai* (elder brothers). At the local or village level, there are equally people in charge of coordinating the activities. None of these persons is really "elected" by any structured organ. Yet, they seem to be fully trusted by the other members of the family.

Swadhyayee's "Achievements"?

The reader may still be tempted to ask the classical question: leaving aside the philosophical considerations, what have these people done exactly, in terms of "economic" or other improvements in their living conditions, which could be concretely evaluated?

To answer this question in the way an "evaluation expert" from an important international "assistance" organization may do, could only provide us with some "data" on a particular dimension of Swadhyaya's overall "achievements," perhaps its least interesting ones. For the purpose of this movement has never really been to "achieve" particular "targets" of a fragmented nature. Neither has it been to deploy concentrated efforts on a specific "project" of interest to a government or a given population, without thinking in advance about the side-effects of that particular project on other life fronts.

This being said, a "development" observer will be surprised to find out that the "economic achievements" of Swadhyaya alone can be most favourably compared to anything achieved by conventional "development" programmes in similar fields.

Before giving a very brief review of such discrete "achievements," the fact has been observed by many a serious outsider[9] that, as a rule, a Swadhyayee village stands clearly against a non-Swadhyayee village, in terms of cleanliness, efficiency and general atmosphere of conviviality and mutual cooperation.[10] I was extremely impressed by a visit done to a large number of Swadhyayee homes in the Daman, Bombay and Gujarat areas, the lively expressions in people's faces, particularly women, and the very visible economic prosperity of these villages cannot remain unnoticed. The size of this paper makes it almost impossible to convey the extent of the transformations I have witnessed in Swadhyayee villages in terms of people's relations with each other, in particular men/women relationships. In my view, these remain by far the most exceptional achievements of the movement.

In terms of more "target-oriented" activities, the following are some of the original and more visible realizations.

Yogeshwar Krushis

A *Yogeshwar Krushi* (God's farm) is a medium size plot of land (three to five acres), where the productive work is performed by volunteers who spend there one or two days in a cropping season. Six to ten *pujarees* (devotees) are, thus, always there, coming from the surrounding villages. The resulting crop which "belongs only to God" becomes part of the "impersonal wealth" produced by the Swadhyayees. One third of the income is used to meet short term needs of the indigents identified by the motabhais of the communities concerned. Although there is a tacit understanding that the sums so distributed are gifts of God and therefore create no obligaton for the recipient to return the money, this *is* returned whenever the latter is in a better economic situation. Giving and receiving of these sums is done so discreetly and with such grace that it obviates any sense of inferiority on the part of the recipients.[11]

The remaining two-thirds of the income is kept locally in a reserve to meet the long-term needs of the community and to buy needed agricultural inputs.

There are now over 3000 Yogeshwar Krushis, and their number is fastly increasing. They differ in may ways from all other collective farms such as they exist in the Soviet Union, China, Israel or even India (the *gramdans*). One main difference is that their members work neither for themselves nor for the group. And their output belonging to no one but God, it is not redistributed amongst the producers, thus avoiding possible conflicts of interests.

The Tree Temples

Tree temples, also called *Upvans* (God's orchards), are new places of reunion and worship where people harness their *nipudata* (creativity/efficiency) at the service of tree planting, the old Vedic tradition considering that trees are a living testament of the omnipresence of God. The upvans are much larger plots of land, which the Swadhyayees of the nearby villages have transformed into beautiful lush green orchards. Because of the "sacred" relationship which ties each tree to the individual or the family which has planted it, the survival rate of plants is claimed to be 100 per cent. The first upvan, named after Valmiki, the author of the epic Ramayan, was raised in 1979. They are now fifteen, and they are likely to increase in an exponential manner. To spend only a day in one of these living tree temples gives an idea of the contagious atmosphere of productive conviviality permeating them. Rich and poor, people of different castes and of former enemy neighbourhoods, come there every day with their families, imparting their Bhakti to their god-inhabited trees. "A work of that magnitude under the official social forestry scheme," report Raman Srivastava and Ramashray Roy, "costs million of rupees, with high casualty rate of plants and numerous complaints against it from those who are supposed to be their beneficiaries."[11]

The Floating Temples

The "carnivorous" fishermen of the coasts of Gujarat and Maharashtra, once considered as the lowest of the low, devoted the fruits of their Bhakti to the creation of floating temples or *matsyagandhas*. The name refers to the first incarnation of God Vishnu as a fish. Here again, the idea started with a number of fishermen (Dada calls them *sagarputras* or sons of the sea) who knew only how to fish and to navigate. Dada suggested that they offer their Bhakti by setting a day's fish of their catch in a month for buying motorised boats, tools and tackles.

Although the experiment is only eight years old, the impersonal wealth, thus produced has already enabled the fishermen to buy over 14 boats. These sons of the sea go now in crews of six to ten persons, to produce impersonal wealth on a systematic basis. Fishing goes on almost round the year except for a three month pause during the monsoon period, used for repairs and refitting the boats. The volunteers are so numerous that no individual fisherman gets a chance for more than a trip in a year.

If one considers that the fishermen in question were once specialising in smuggling, gambling and committing petty or major crimes, most of them fighting each other, it is almost unbelievable how their new swadhyayee perception of reality has transformed their lives. Their regenerated creative abilities (*nipudata*) has not only helped them to become more beautiful human beings, but also to produce the impersonal wealth which has made most of them, now, economically prosperous and self-reliant.[12]

The Many Other Bouquets of Bhakti

In a talk Dadaji gave to some 300,000 swadhyayees while he was given the Gandhi Award in January 1988, he made it clear that Swadhyaya was not undertaken "to solve all the problems of the world. We are merely planting," he said, "a bouquet of flowers of love and compassion, selflessness and peace."

The bouquets, such things as Yogeshwar Krushi, tree temples and floating temples, may be enough to give a first idea of the fragrance of the many flowers regenerated by the Swadhyaya stream. Much larger a space would be needed to describe all the others. To convey a more comprehensive idea of their great diversity, it would however be fair to mention at least the following:

• *Amrutalayam* (hut-temples or, literally, respositories of divine nectar), are another living temple conceived by Dada. Here, under the thatched or locally produced roof of a simple construction, often surrounded by small beautiful gardens, all of which have been built by the villagers, the latter assemble every evening, irrespective of caste or creed. After prayers are offered to the Yogeshwar (as a rule, represented by the holy family of Krishna on the right of the altar, Ganesh and Parvati in the middle, and Shiva on the left), some Swadhyayees recite their Geeta, others perhaps their Bible or Qor'an. Individual and collective problems are discussed informally. Offerings are made anonymously with a view to increasing the impersonal wealth of the village. Amrutalayam are now the new socio-cultural centres of activity in most villages where 80 percent have joined the parivar. They have become the focus of an alternative world of learning and social life independent of the state which has begun to lay claim on controlling them.[11]

• *Vayastha-Sanchalans* are gatherings of individuals 18 to 40 years of age who, irrespective of caste, creed or status, get together to exchange their experiences. In turn, they help organize the community celebrations of *ustavs* (festivals), *teerth yatras* (pilgrimages) and *yagnas* (ritualistic religious ceremonies). Each of these activities are an opportunity for "the sacred and not-sacred to wholly merge. The essential worship becomes self-transformation which, in turn, is related to the transformation of the community."[11]

• In the educational field, *Tattvajnana Vidyapeeth* (Centre for learning the ultimate knowledge), was one of the first learning institutions created by Dada in 1965. It provides nonformal graduate education in Vedic and some modern education subjects. "The education that is provided lays more stress on self-development than on the student merely acquiring an ability for improving financial position."[4]

• An "Association for the Spread of Vedic Culture" (*Sanskruti Vistarak Sangh*) coordinates and oversees activities related to bhaktiferis and other Swadhyayee activities.

• Four nonformal schools, of which three provide secondary level and one college level education, are managed under a central body called Jnana Vistarak Sangh (Association for the Spread of Knowledge). A special feature of these schools is the incursion of farming as an important subject. Theoretical and practical training is given in agriculture. Graduates of these schools go back to their community and become very active members of their villages. More recently a Centre for vocational training has been opened for children of tribals, near Baroda.

• *Bal Sanskar Kendra* (Children's centres) are "character building centres for young boys and girls." Children, generally up to 15 years of age, gather here every day to learn how to develop their divine capacities according to the spirit of Vedic culture and traditions. These centres which now run into several thousands are "animated" by volunteers under the supervision of a young Swadhyayee teacher responsible for the curricular and extra-curricular activities.

• *Bahna Kendras* (Sisters' centres) are designed to help Swadhyayee sisters to teach and help each other in domestic skills. Much of their activities revolve around village life, and daily problems of the villagers, particularly women.

As a whole, these bouquets of Swadhyaya have been created out of needs felt at the local level. When their success is appreciated by other Swadhyayees, similar activities start elsewhere. Only when they become quantitatively important, Dada envisages the possibility of providing them with an "umbrella organization." But even so, they remain highly decentralized and, to this date, not bureaucratized at all.

An example of this type of "endogenous development" in the "economic" field started with the creation, somewhere, of a parivar store for the sale of surplus produce of Swadhyayee villages like grains, pulses, edible and non-edible oils, soaps, match sticks, candles, milk products, etc. Response to this initiative was so great that such stores, actually named Parivars, were seen mushrooming everywhere in a very short period. The same could be said of *Gauras* (milk produce centres) which have been recently set up in a few villages for making milk available to villagers and sell the surplus in the form of milk products to outside markets.

Concluding Remarks

It is almost impossible to conclude on this very novel phenomenon of Swadhyaya which seems to have suddenly come into the open, after years of "underground" formation. Yet the kind of heart-to-heart work which started with a few individuals, incubated for almost two decades, and manifested itself in the form of almost unrelated sources and little brooks finding their own little paths, seems to have lately become like a new Ganga, inspiring its riverains with feelings similarly composed of sacred and non-sacred elements. More, this very fast growing stream is quietly watering a silent, yet singing revolution of very original and thought-provoking dimensions.

Indeed, the stream confronts the compassionate observer with a host of questions, many of which need much more time, attention and careful observation to be seriously addressed. Some are questions of a philosophical nature. Some relate to the inevitable limits of such streams in a surrounding world strongly conditioned to respond negatively to them. There are other questions which call for a fresh re-examination of the contradictions inherent to the size limits of creative micro-initiatives. Amongst the many others stands also the dilemma of the "charismatic leader" whose worldview militates in favour of open-ended processes of exploration and self-discovery, yet whose very charismatic presence tends to generate new forms of voluntary servitude toward the leader.

To probe into these questions requires, no doubt, an observant and compassionate mind, particularly free from cliches and the concept proper to the impatient observers of our "development" age, whether they belong to the supporter of the "establishment" or to its critics, some of whom represent only the other side of the coin.

In the meantime, one cannot but rejoice that, in a world where those cliches have already done so much harm to people's inner and outer freedom, there are still a growing number of people who are trying to use their divine intelligence and imagination in bringing their own responses to their sufferings.

Finally, it is particularly refreshing to find out that, despite the systematic and forceful colonization of minds by *homo economicus* and the modern institutions operating for him, there are still millions of people who refuse to be addicted by him, desperately trying to reconcile their pressing material needs with their aspirations as free and dignified human beings. It is also, perhaps, a significant sign of the times to come that in such a situation, a religious mind like Dada invites the same millions, in the very name of traditions to "get liberated from our pre-conceived ideas and opinions and baseless beliefs. . . . As we put off our clothes while taking bath," says this contemporary son of the Vedic seers, "likewise let us leave aside our traditional ideas and think and discuss rationally, keeping our mind free."[2]

Notes and References

1. Ramashray Roy and R.K. Srivastava are two scholars who have undertaken a comprehensive study of Swadhyaya for the United Nations University, to be published soon. I owe a debt of gratitude to both these colleagues and friends. Raman Srivastava, in particular, has spent long periods of time in Swadhyayee villages. It is thanks to him that it became possible, for me to meet Dadaji and to be warmly welcomed everywhere by the Swadhyayee parivar. R.R. and R.K.S. kindly provided me with the manuscript of the main chapters of their study for the UNU.

2. Pandurang Shastri Athavale, *Light That Leads*. Lectures delivered by the author (Bombay: Sat Vichar Darshan, 1987).

3. To avoid possible confusion and misunderstanding, it is important to bear in mind that the term "religion" has a different connotation here. Particularly in Non-Muslim India, it is *not* associated with a belief or faith in a number of pre-defined and unquestionable dogmas. On the contrary, it presents an open-ended search for Truth in all its manifestations. Religion is generally synonymous with Dharma. The latter is a moral order, an order which expresses the law of living, sustaining and upholding the Cosmos. The order is maintained through everyone's acts. Dharma means equally the inner gift and power which enables

us to sustain that order. It means that "every person shall be enabled to become, and by no misdirection prevented from becoming what he has in him to become."

4. All the visitors who attended this extraordinary meeting, talk about it in superlative terms. R.K. Srivastava was impressed, amongst other things, by the fact that, despite Dada's refusal to invite the police commissioner of the area for the security arrangements of the meeting, the festival had become a spiritual manifestation of brotherhood, that took itself care of all its many unforeseen events. Allahabad is, however, a place where "criminal acts and petty thefts are common during pilgrim's gatherings." For a short and vivid description of the gathering, see *Swadhyaya and Its Activities: A Synopsis*, published in 1988 by Sat Vichar Darshan, Bombay, pp. 79-94.

5. In his discourses, Dada often expresses his general agreement with the concept of alienation, as developed by Hegel and Marx. Yet, he believes the concept should be expanded further. "Man, he says, produced machines and many more things. Now they are dominating over man. Marx's idea of alienation in this context is very illuminating. . . . According to this view, man is belittled. Things and machines are overvalued. . . . Marx says: Man is lost. The ancient seers said: the indwelling Lord is lost sight of. These two ways of thinking are closely related to each other. Vedant says the same thing."

6. Dada has a genius for putting at ease "ordinary" people, in particular the downtrodden and those who are socially looked down by others. He invites them to feel proud about their "difference," rather than feeling bad about it. To the porters, he says that Krishna was a porter. To the fisherman, he says that Vishnu reincarnated as a fish. To the "untouchables," he says: only those are *achyut* or "untouchable" who have not been "touched" by the grace of the God within them. Rather than condemning or reprimanding anyone for what he or she does or has done, he seeks to reassure everyone that awareness of the God within is always enough for starting a new life. This approach has most efficiently served Swadhyayees in changing people's lives where everyone else, even the Gandhians, had failed. The following two cases are worth mentioning in this context:

a) Facharia is a village in Gujarat where the majority of people were drunkards, "outlaws" and fighters indulging in liquor trafficking, drug sales and criminal offenses. Since they have joined the Swadhyaya family, their lives have completely changed. Presently, it is a village of peaceful agriculturists which Dada has re-named Gokul, after a pious ancient city where Krishna himself had decided to reside.

b) In Porbandar, Gandhiji's birthplace, long mafia-type relations of feud and violence had always opposed the Khawar and the Mer communities. While officials had given up trying to control the situation and jails could no longer contain the offenders, the patient work of Swadhyayees put an end to decades of violence, murders and criminal activities. On 21 March 1984, two thousand couples from the warring factions sat and sung together, in Dada's presence. (See *Swadhyaya and its Activities*, pp. 61-72 and 73-78. Also Dr. Vern Barnet, *Dada's Message and Methods*, excerpts from Remarks at the Lenexa Community Centre, 3 May 1986).

7. This is the title of an earlier book in English, containing a collection of Dada's discourses. See Shastri Shri Athavale, *Thoughts on Glorious Heritage* (Bombay: Sat Vichar Darshan, 1975).

8. See, in particular, the translation in English of Dadaji's discourse on the occasion of the Diamond Jubilee Celebration of Shrimad Bhagvad Geeta Patshala, Bombay, 10 January 1988.

9. Shri R.K. Srivastava, *Swadhyaya Movement: Its Meaning and Message*, a mimeographed paper presented at the UN Seminar in Rome (September 1986) p.11.

10. See also Betty M. Unterberger, transcript of a radio interview, 1986.

11. Ramashray Roy and R.K. Srivastava, Manuscript of the Study for UNU, p. 349.

12. I was particularly impressed by my visit to a village in the Daman region. The economic prosperity of this village was a direct result of the changes which had transformed people's psychology and general attitudes toward life, particularly in their relationships with each other. There, more than anywhere else, I realized that Swadhyaya was a silent yet singing revolution. Hundreds of songs have been improvised by the members of this great family. Many of them were sung during the whole day the author spent on board of a *Matsyagandha*, in company of joyful and enthusiastic Swadhyayee fishermen.

Chapter Eight:
Helping Children Become Good Adults In a Complex World

by Joseph Schaeffer

His background. College professor and international researcher in anthropology, communication and social issues. Musical director, composer and pianist for theatrical performances including television, off-Broadway and national tours. Fluent in English, Spanish, French and German. Occasional lecturer and audiovisual consultant. Pastimes include contacting and interviewing leading world thinkers on the fundamental issues of all ages. His many published works range in subject from the use of videotape in anthropology to the smoking of cannabis and ganja among Jamaicans. Ph.D., Anthropology (Columbia)

His chapter. In recent years has interviewed dozens of the world's leading thinkers in the quest for sensible answers that will guide us safely toward a new century and a new age of human development. The opening pages of his chapter put our lives and world into perspective with our evolution from ancestral roots before providing six provocative answers to what may be the most compelling question of any era: What should we be doing with today's children so that they become good ancestors for future generations?

We must teach children a degree of flexibility, but not to the extent that the world seems to be chaotic.

Helping Children Become
Good Adults in a Complex World

by Joseph Schaeffer

Each age of humanity has a particular position in the narrative history of the species. That position can be characterized uniquely. At the same time it is confined within past and future stories.

Each age of humanity has its problems. Over and over again human beings, within the limits of their biological capacities, must meet the challenge of cultural, social, economic, and political life in the natural environment.

Each age of humanity has knowledge or qualities of comprehension. Knowledge carries the potential for understanding and choice in human activity.

The several ages in our human ancestry begin with the nomadic hunter-gatherers who roamed the lands first in Africa and later in Asia, Europe, and the Americas. A second age is characterized by early sedentism when groups of hunter-gatherers settled along seaways and in riverine environments, particularly in Southern Europe, Asia, and North America.

The development of large-scale agriculture with its complex social-economic-political-religious patterns and practices in the Nile, Tigres-Euphrates, and Indus River basins marks the beginning of the third age. The central characteristic of the third age was expansionism. We see this in the massive growth of the population of the species, the migration of that population into the far corners of the globe, and the discovery of extraordinary technologies for the exploitation and use of the natural environment. During its ten thousand years the third age also witnessed the development and consolidation of lifeways, of social, economic, political patterns and processes, characterized by rigid hierarchies of authority and prestige, authoritarianism, combative competition, often violent conflict, a preoccupation with order, materialism, and the rise of science culminating in the industrial revolution and World War II.

The changes in the size and distribution of the population combined with the explosion in technology generated unexpected problems including overpopulation in particular areas, the depletion of resources, deadening pollution, the extinction of a variety of plant and animal species, economic instability, and widespread poverty. And the conflictive, competitive lifeways led to social discrimination, economic injustice, and political repression in many areas of the world. These problems are gravitous indeed. In the context of a global society organized into states characterized by national chauvinism they become potentially disastrous.

We are now entering a fourth age brought on by discoveries which give us the ability to interfere with matter at the level of atomic structure and to manipulate genetic processes at the very foundation of life, by the development of communication technology which makes it possible for all areas of the world to interact, and by a growing awareness that the globe has systemic limits, that its resources are not unending, that it cannot sustain expansion forever.

The narrative history of the fourth age is already being written in prospect by visionary historians who imagine a society characterized by an acceptance of complexity, creative conflict without violence, independence and regional control in a context of interdependence and exchange, and a reasonable and responsible distribution of wealth and power. In this society institutions will be humane as well as pragmatic. We will turn to the humanities and the arts as well as science to understand and explain human actions. Large-scale and small-scale societies will interact without becoming homogeneous. Modern and traditional ways of thinking will exist side by side. We will witness the intertwining of material needs and human values. And we will use the resources in the environment from a perspective of interdependence. Aspects of this society are described in the works of contemporary scholars from a variety of fields including Kenneth Boulding (*The World as a Total System*), David Bohm (*Wholeness and the Implicate Order*), C. West Churchman, (*Thought and Wisdom*), Riane Eisler (*The Chalice and the Blade*), Buckminster Fuller (*Synergetics*),

Erich Jantsch (*The Self-Organizing Universe*), Leopold Kohr (*The Breakdown of Nations*), George Lakoff (*Women, Fire, and Dangerous Things*), Ilya Prigogine and Isabelle Stengers (*Order Out of Chaos*), Jonas Salk (*The Survival of the Wisest*), and Lynn Segal (*The Dream of Reality*), among others.

The problems of the fourth age include those carried over from the past age of expansionism. In addition we face new problems which accompany the discoveries in nuclear physics and biology, the possibility of nuclear conflagration and the potential for irreversible and possibly lethal changes in natural evolutionary processes. We must also recognize a less evident though equally serious problem brought on with innovative communication technology on a shrinking planet. This problem has to do with the necessity for exchange across cultural boundaries and with it the need for an understanding of human interaction in decision-making processes in international negotiation.

The qualities of comprehension available to us today, as is so often the case in the evolution of our species, are those that can best serve the visionary history and the problems of our times. These qualities of comprehension come from quantum theory in physics, chaos theory in mathematics, sociobiology, learning theory, studies of intelligence, cognitive semantics, human ecology, general systems theory, negotiation theory, and studies of myth and religion. Quantum theory points up the intimate relation between the observer and the observed and the inevitable unpredictability of changes in quanta. Chaos theory allows us the confidence that in seemingly random phenomena we can find order. Sociobiology reminds us of the interplay between biology and culture in human choice. Cognitive semantics elucidates the relation between our sense of reality and the nature of symbolic life in language. Learning theory gives us an understanding of our capacity for perspective. Human ecology and general systems theory emphasize the structure and organization of all systems including societies. Negotiation theory asks us to explore cultural differences and similarities in decision-making. And studies of myth and religion give us a sense of human universals in prehistory and history.

Taken together these qualities of comprehension point to an innovative, pluralistic, integrative, interactive, unified universe at all levels, in all its complexities. They lead to certain values in human society, perhaps even an ethic, a basis for moral decisions, emphasizing creativity and empathy, individual potential and mutuality, and variety and unity.

Given this scenario it is clear that once again, as with all ages and at any point in time, we stand at a pinnacle in history. And it behooves us to raise the perennial questions that must be raised in every age, among them: What should we be doing with children today so that they become good ancestors for future generations?

I have posed this question and others to many of the true heroes of our time—people concerned with such fundamental questions. The individuals I have contacted accept human nature in human culture, realizing that blind membership in society is no longer safe. They learn from the past and envision the future as they live in the present. They act on the available knowledge while remaining open to new knowledge. They accept the responsibility to establish a meaningful ethic in a world of paradox. And they are fully conscious members in the evolution of the universe.

We live in what many people believe to be the most frightening of times. One of my interviewees said to me that she chose not to have children because she could not guarantee what the world of the future would be like. I don't understand this position. Our children have the possibility of living in a world we can only dream of, in a cooperative, integrative, planetary society. Our joy, and it is a joy to savor, is in the transition to that world. "Power," wrote Emerson, "ceases in the instant of repose; it resides in the moment of transition from a past to a new state, in the shooting of the gulf, in the darting of an aim." (Emerson, *Self-Reliance*)

Following are a few of the replies I have received to the question, "What should we be doing with children today so that they become good ancestors for future generations?"

David Bohm
Professor of Physics (Emeritus) Birkbeck College, University of London, and well-known author.

We must make sure we don't dampen the possibility of creativity in children. Each society's aim is to prepare children to enter into that society. "Training" methods are geared to accomplish this goal. Unfortunately, these methods generally produce mechanical behavior. This is very dangerous because it leads to conformity and repetitiousness.

There is a basic distinction between creativity and mechanicalness. Mechanicalness is fundamentally destructive in the long run. Societies usually decay and collapse because they accumulate mechanical ways of thinking. There are many signs that this is happening in our society. We have to look for ways to stop the trend.

Body Cells or Beasts?

A biosystem like the body is incredibly well organized inside. The overall collective aim of all the members (cells, tissues, organs) is to maintain peace, order and security at all levels. Cells fit into specialized roles with no chance of retraining and job hunting. They seem to have neither the need nor the desire for variety in their lives, and they certainly don't seem to get much.

An ecosystem like a forest or ocean is incredibly disorganized inside. There is no underlying collective aim of the members (wild animals and plants). Each member's overriding individual aim is to survive. Doing so means eating other members of the ecosystem and protecting oneself, in turn, from being eaten. If peace, order and security typify the inside of a biosystem, then conflict, chaos and insecurity are the rule inside an ecosystem.

The inside of a social system such as a city or nation is characterized by a mix of peace and conflict, order and disorder, security and insecurity. It is like a hybrid cross between a biosystem and an ecosystem. We humans, the members of social systems, are like living cells in some regards and like wild animals in others. Part of us wants the security of a well-organized social system for protection while another part pulls us toward a life of excitement and unpredictability.

Joseph Schaeffer's interviewees in Chapter 8 express concern that modern schools try to mold children to be alike and to behave mechanically, a bit like cells. They, like Robert Muller in Chapter 10, advocate a balance — teaching a basic framework of crucial knowledge (like Mr. Muller's World Core Curriculum) while fostering creativity and free thinking, and helping individual students to recognize and bolster their unique, innate strengths.

If the purpose of life is to bring order to an otherwise chaotic, entropic universe, then education is the means by which we humans can do our part, broadening knowledge of our planet, our societies and ourselves.

—*MHM*

There are no easy prescriptions, no formula, for creativity. Prescriptions, in fact, would be inconsistent with creativity. We can be reasonably sure, however, that if adults are not creative it's going to be hard for children to learn to be creative. And there are a few things we can say about such things as rewards, control, challenge, and accomplishment that are relevant to creativity.

Margaret Drabble
Well-known novelist living in London.

Children need, first, to learn affection, love, emotional connection. Parents need to communicate these to children and to receive them back from children. Most damaged people have not experienced affection or security in a two-way process as small children. They don't establish the habit of affection.

I include physical affection here as well—the ability to relate physically, remembering that we are bodies as well as minds. Babies need to be picked up, children need to be kissed. Aging mothers need to be kissed by their aging children. We must establish and maintain a natural physical communion in our families.

Beyond this, I think we have to recognize the stages in a child's individuality. We have to know that the child is not a replica. He is developing interests, developing individual qualities that need to be encouraged. We must allow him to be different from us.

Ervin Laszlo
Philosopher, general systems theorist, author of over 50 books and 200 articles, member of the Club of Rome, a Fellow of the United Nations Institute for Training and Research, and a Distinguished Tutor of the International College.

I think we must do a combination of things. We must not only give children facts. We must not tell them that a given system of knowledge is a system of facts, take it or leave it. Every system of knowledge is mutable. We must live with this. We must teach children a degree of openness and flexibility so that they have room for learning. At the same time, we must not do this to such an extent that the world seems to be chaotic—a place in which anything goes, in which any system of knowledge is as good as any other.

Somewhere between absolute dogmatism and total relativism there is an optimum place where a child feels that he has some key concepts, some key ideas with which he can work. But these are always changing as he elaborates upon them, adapts to outside influences, discovers related ideas, and tests them in action. So he must remain flexible, teaching himself in a changing environment at the same time as he molds the environment to his needs and requirements. The outcome of this process, we may hope, is a satisfactory life.

A child starts with certain codes or perceptual mechanisms whereby he takes in the world around him, perceives it, and then organizes it. But his perceptions can harden in a single channel, or they can diversify. If they harden in a single channel, he gradually becomes more and more narrow-minded and dogmatic. If, on the other hand, they become too diverse, he launches off in too many directions indiscriminately. There is too much trial and error, and he becomes confused, disoriented, and even, perhaps, superficial.

One of the tasks of a parent and an educator should be to note the areas in which a child shows a distinct interest and then to help him or her develop in that area. At the same time, he must stimulate the child to look into other areas, to explore different perspectives, so the child doesn't get stuck in one thing.

To achieve this goal, there are many options in formal educational systems dealing with younger children including open classrooms, experiential learning, or hands-on learning, for example. Whatever the option, it is important that education be tailored to meet the needs of each individual child. A child's pathways are reasonably free and self-organizing. The educational system must reflect this. Once the child has lived and experienced a phenomenon (a process), he can then learn what he needs to know to explain it. He can learn theory. Later he can learn to connect experience and theory on his own. But my first concern, even more than as an educator, is as a father to provide an intellectual input which keeps a child and then a young person open, but which, at the same time, equips him to cope with this openness—to keep it from degenerating into chaos.

Victor Weisskopf
Professor of Physics (Emeritus) at M.I.T., author of many books and articles, and a former president of the American Academy of Sciences.

The schooling in the United States is inadequate because it is not directed toward personal interest, toward what I call wonder. In *Knowledge and Wonder* I quote Francis Bacon: "Wonder is the source of culture." But too often our children are not taught to wonder, to discover, to play around in a guided way. They are taught by rote and their interest is deadened rather than awakened.

The strange idea exists that knowledge is knowing answers. Actually, knowledge is knowing what questions to ask. Especially in this country education is considered to be just the accumulation of facts. That's not at all right. Teachers should not teach facts. They should teach thinking. They should encourage children to ask questions. Then they should show them where they can find the answers to their questions. Library use should be a required course, even in elementary school.

I used to say that you should not cover a subject, you should uncover part of it. You should take part of a subject and teach it in depth instead of trying to cover everything. Indeed, I remember that when I was in school I could only learn if I first created a vacuum in my head. You cannot press knowledge into the heads of children. You have to create a vacuum so that the knowledge is sucked in. How do you create a vacuum? By engendering interest.

Jean Freymond
Director, Center for Applied Studies in International Negotiations, Geneva, Switzerland.

Parents and schools must share responsibility in the raising and education of children. Parents as well as teachers must be prepared for this responsibility. But part of the process is reversed. That is, children also educate and raise parents and teachers. They do this more now than they did in the past and they will do it even more in the future.

Secondly, we must put much more emphasis on the primary school level than on the secondary school level. The capacity of children to absorb before the age of ten or twelve, before they get into their teens, is much greater than we think. Yet we usually tend to load knowledge into the later years. We should reverse the process.

Thirdly, we must rethink the traditional focus on disciplines. Ask first what are the skills the child needs to feel confident in any given society and to be able to adjust to life in that society. Communication is a necessary skill. Children must learn to listen carefully and to speak and write clearly in their own language. Then they should learn to do so in at least two other languages.

Children also need a sense of self-identity to adjust in their society. One way to help them achieve this is to organize the things they learn in such a way that they understand their place that they belong—in this complex world.

Charles Burdick
Dean of Faculty, School of Social Sciences, San Jose State University, San Jose, California.

First and foremost in my view is nurturing. Nurturing involves a complex human relationship. It is essential to survival. It takes human children longer to reach maturity than any other animal in our world. You have to nurture them into the sense of continuity which is fundamental to humankind. You want them to have curiosity, to know that there is a world beyond their understanding that has to be pursued. You want them to be considerate of other human beings. This is fundamental to our existence. Since we have to have some kind of exchange you want to nurture them in the sense of a world beyond them. And you want to give them a feeling for religious values in the cultural sense. This is highly important. You want them to understand that man cannot, will not, ever master his environment. Children have to understand this very early in life. Too often we think we can control or dominate our environment. This has led us now into terrible pitfalls.

A second fundamental thing with children has to do with an understanding of reality. Reality includes the hard knocks of life: winning and losing, suffering and pleasure, control and lack of control, emotion and intellect, all kinds of contradictions which one should approach early and quickly.

A third fundamental part of childhood must include order and discipline. These, of course, are part of nurturing. I choose to list them here because they are forces which young people must confront and seldom on their terms.

Children have to learn to be adults early without the dilemmas and difficulties of adulthood. We miss some of that today in our rearing of young children. We turn them into middle age before they reach puberty. That's an awesome responsibility. We wonder why they bail out and go to drugs and all kinds of other things. They have nothing to look forward to, no future which they are part of and which they can enjoy. It is fundamental to them that life can be fun.

Part III:
Healing the Planet

Love blends together the many levels of life—allowing cells to operate smoothly as biosystems like the body . . . and helping individuals to work and play together happily as social systems. As we move toward a new century and a new age, love is boiling over into the higher levels, helping social systems function together as a cohesive planet.

The force called love is generated by the Holy Spirit or divine essence or kundalini or shakti or Qi or life energy, which surges through our bodies.

Planetary healing will be a boiling-over of personal and social healing. As individuals let love fire up their hearts and as massive social systems—nations, religions, transnational corporations and regional ecosystems—start working together rather than against each other, the world will be in a healing mode.

Love, in short, can heal the earth. "And what an incredible Earth it is, turning at 1,666 kilometers per hour with so much life on it, with people standing on it, their heads pointing like antennae into all directions of the universe, with leaves, plants and algae avidly absorbing the sun's energy!" exalts one of this book's authors. (Robert Muller in *Most of All, They Taught Me Happiness*, World Happiness and Cooperation, 1989)

Many leading-edge thinkers driven by love of planet are now putting together solutions for our troubled world. Among them:

Hazel Henderson explains how healing the planet will require replacing the ecologically destructive realities of economic theory with a new means of monitoring society's well-being that takes into account such factors as the environment and loving, unpaid services such as parenting.

Robert Muller shows that we are on the verge of a wonderful new era of love, interdependence and mutual respect. Arriving there will require global education that fosters wholesome values and universal understanding in an entire young generation.

John McDonald explains that citizen diplomacy. can help erase barriers between societies, but to be effective a citizen diplomat needs to learn certain do's and don'ts.

Keith Suter shows how the planet cannot be healed as long as national interests take priority over global interests on topsoil, rainforests, oceans, atmosphere, space and other critical subjects that span the borders and determine the well-being of many countries.

Hilkka Pietila shows that at the core of planetary healing must be sustainable development—a new means of growth and sustenance of societies which ensures environmental integrity.

Chapter Nine:
Beyond Economics

by Hazel Henderson

Her background. Independent futurist, author, television producer and moderator, freelance journalist. Advisor, consultant and lecturer for universities, foundations, nonprofit organizations, governments, and corporations in over 30 countries. Many affiliations as advisor, director, member, fellow, trustee, including WorldWatch Institute, the Cousteau Society, the Lindisfarne Association, The Elmwood Institute, Findhorn Foundation, Global Education Associates, East-West University. Her world-changing efforts began as volunteer work in 1967 when, refusing to raise her young daughter in ever-denser New York smog, she founded Citizens for Clean Air, Inc., which earned her the New York Medical Society's Citizen of the Year award. Currently she is travelling the world, conferring with world leaders.

Her chapter. Traditional economics operates as though the world consists only of self-interested, mutually distrustful nations and individuals. It has lost touch with the real things—love, generosity and voluntary efforts to help others. Meanwhile, we are becoming more interdependent and cooperative as we move toward a win-win world of sustainable development. Concern for others and for the environment, long the cornerstone of many poor countries, is clearly needed now by the overdeveloped world ... and economists had better step out of people's way as they pursue it.

It is time to retrain economists or replace them with systems theorists, futurists, ecologists, and other interdisciplinary advisors.

Beyond Economics

by Hazel Henderson

Today a new era is dawning in the world—the Age of Interdependence. Bewildering uncertainties are now affecting most people, whether Americans, Russians, Chinese or others, as human societies restructure and align themselves in the many global transformation processes now occurring. There are at least seven great globalization processes changing all our lives:
- Production and technology
- Employment, work and migration
- Finance, debt and information (which has become interchangeable with money)
- The arms race and militarization,
- Global pollution and resource depletion
- Culture and consumption, and
- The multiple realignments and restructurings driven by the prior six globalization processes.

These processes are circular and interactive, they are accelerating due to their interactivity, and they are irreversible.

Living in the Past

Traditional western economics is living in a bygone era, ignoring these processes and operating under the illusion that we are all rational, competitive individuals with very little tendency toward group cooperation. Emphasis is on self-interest of individuals and nations.

Nations and multinational corporations construct their values and goals around this notion of self-interest, and they all try to maximize their gains in no-holds-barred competition. There is a general avoidance of difficult or troublesome questions, such as what sort of behavior will produce a healthy planet for our descendants. In the 1300s English villages had a "commons area" in which everyone grazed their sheep. Following their competitive instincts, the villagers began to maximize their personal gain by allowing their sheep to overgraze in the area. And the commons were eventually destroyed. Today's international competition is based on a similarly dangerous perception of reality. Nations, competing in their political policies and economic goals, are digging ravenously into the *global* commons to acquire resources. This shortsightedness is undermining the environment and the global economy itself.

Fortunately, perceptions are changing at the grassroots level of society. Today we realize that we need each other, and because of that our self-interests in the long run are all identical. While economic theory doesn't acknowledge this interdependence, many people are starting to live more simply, fighting to protect the environment, consuming less, feeling a sense of kinship and warm bond with other individuals and companies that are globally concerned.

It is just as natural for people to behave cooperatively in their day-to-day social activities as to behave competitively. Even in economies like the US, which are primarily competitive, there is a stable foundation of trust and cooperation upon which everything else is built. Trust within organizations, clubs and companies, trust between buyers and suppliers, cooperation and trust among different companies and communities and states. And trust among nations that work together on treaties and agreements to solve mutual problems or that form long-term trade relationships.

Economic theory ignores all the unpaid, loving, cooperative, voluntary work in homes, in neighborhoods and in communities that provides the vital framework for society. Competitive, traditional economics ignores this "love economy" and Mother Nature's "work" precisely *because* it is unpaid and unaccounted for in national statistics and indicators like the gross national product (GNP).

As illustrated in Figure 1, the total economy is like a three-layer cake with icing. The icing is the private sector with its productivity, innovation and freedom. It rests above the public sector, which is also a productive sector. Both of these top layers rest on the informal, cooperative sector . . . and at the bottom, supporting the entire cake, is Mother Nature.

Money Is Information

Money is a symbol, nothing more, nothing less. We often make far too much of it; sometimes maybe too little. Money provides a valuable service to society only if it tracks accurately the relationships among people, products, services and natural resources.

Traditional economists tend to look at life as an equation, with money on one side and, say, products, resources and jobs on the other side. By traditional definitions, any form of economic activity will create jobs. One can dig a million holes in the ground and then fill them back up, which will change nothing. One can build a factory that produces weapons that will make the world a more dangerous place to live. One can build a factory that produces food to help the people of the world. One can wage a war on drugs or fight to educate people—activities that make society healthier. All these activities will create jobs. What we need to do now is to carefully analyze what is needed in our changing world, what societies need, and then define the projects and jobs which will satisfy those needs. It might be mentioned that the most important job in any society is parenting and socializing our children. And in most societies it is essentially an unpaid job.

Modern economics has strayed away from this close relationship with real, natural things, and the world's abstract financial system has become unstable as governments manipulate money supplies. We are approaching a sort of voodoo economics in which money is becoming all important and the natural materials and activities it represents are being neglected. Bewildering new forms of abstract assets and trading methods are being created. Government policy makers look to economists for help but are given only these abstractions and symptomatic illusions. Central bankers believe they have only two options—tightening up the money supply and risking recession on one hand, or loosening the money supply and risking inflation on the other.

Economies have grown centralized and unwieldy far beyond the point where such simplistic remedies can help solve the problem. This crisis of perception is clouding our understanding

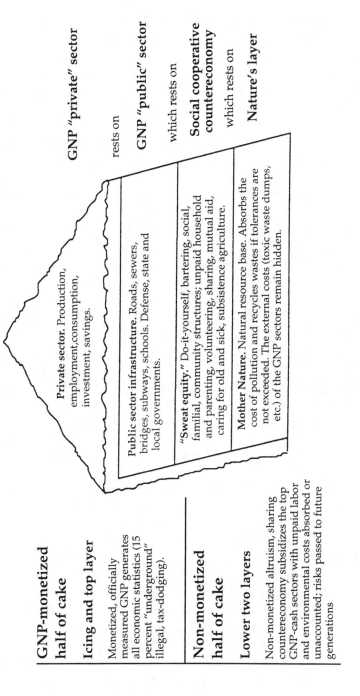

GNP-monetized half of cake

Icing and top layer

Monetized, officially measured GNP generates all economic statistics (15 percent "underground" illegal, tax-dodging).

Non-monetized half of cake

Lower two layers

Non-monetized altruism, sharing countereconomy subsidizes the top GNP-cash sectors with unpaid labor and environmental costs absorbed or unaccounted; risks passed to future generations

GNP "private" sector

rests on

GNP "public" sector

which rests on

Social cooperative countereconomy

which rests on

Nature's layer

Private sector. Production, employment, consumption, investment, savings.

Public sector infrastructure. Roads, sewers, bridges, subways, schools. Defense, state and local governments.

"Sweat equity." Do-it-yourself, bartering, social, familial, community structures; unpaid household and parenting, volunteering, sharing, mutual aid, caring for old and sick, subsistence agriculture.

Mother Nature. Natural resource base. Absorbs the cost of pollution and recycles wastes if tolerances are not exceeded. The external costs (toxic waste dumps, etc.) of the GNP sectors remain hidden.

Figure 1   **Total Production System of an Industrial Society (Three-layer cake with icing)**

of the fundamental transformation of today's social systems, as each restructures itself to fit the world's new, interdependent nature. This re-perception of whole systems and restructuring of our knowledge is really the only way out of our economic dilemma. Governments must break the shackles of modern economics and develop new values and goals within the framework of the real world.

Today's governments have at their disposal a wide range of new policy tools. Systems theory, game theory, cross-impact studies, futures research, technology assessments, scenario building, and environmental impact statements. These and other tools move beyond the realm of traditional economics into the more natural world of people, products, resources, human skills, human sentiments and technologies. These and other modern tools fashioned from general systems theory, are now essential for societies in today's world to manage themselves effectively.

The world has grown into a complex web of industries, technologies, migrating peoples, pollution, resource depletion, militarization, finances and culture. Trying to control or regulate this complex web with monetary and fiscal policies measured by single indicators like GNP is like trying to fly a modern jet airliner with nothing but an oil pressure gauge! Using unreliable symbols to regulate the real world can't work, but that's what economists have been attempting with their myopic indicators.

A useful new concept for rethinking old economics is *sustainable development*. In our quest for solutions to today's crises we need to look toward the new models of sustainable development as outlined in the WorldWatch Institute's *State of the World* reports or the Brundtland Report. Traditional policies around the world are leading us to ruin. The conspicuous consumption in the "over" developed countries is leading to depleted resources and energy while environments and the citizenry are being poisoned by chemicals and synthetics.

The less "developed" parts of the world are seeing their forests being stripped away, grasslands overgrazed and hillsides stripped and cultivated, becoming prone to erosion. The poor economies struggle to survive by exporting crops grown on land needed for their own food and by exporting raw materials and commodities at knock-down prices set by powerful countries and abstract world economics. As the land is ruined, people swarm to the cities to join the starving masses.

For healthy social systems to thrive in a healthy world, we need to use more effective methods of taking the pulse of the world and societies—to formulate development policies that can be sustained over the long term by available resources. The main economic indicator of the past—the GNP—still ignores social and environmental conditions and encourages overconsumption. This short-sighted, single economic gauge must be replaced by a full range of instruments that take into account real human concerns—indicators of *true* development. The Country Futures Indicators (Table 1), for example, will enable us to compare *real* progress with *genuinely* sustainable development. Many other new and systematic measurements such as the Physical Quality of Life Index, the Basic Human Needs Index and others using many disciplines are available. Reliance on archaic economic tools such as GNP cripples our ability to heal today's planet.

Once the old economic ideologies such as capitalism, socialism, communism, supply-side economics, and monetarism are transcended, new policies can benefit from systems approaches and multiple feedbacks. Monitoring the rapid changes going on in the world and accepting feedback from citizens (i.e. expanding democracy), from the environment and from other countries—as well as from prices which include the *social* costs for production—will vastly improve policy-making toward a healthy future.

Social systems accepting and utilizing such feedback will learn from their mistakes, make corrections, and continually experiment and evolve. Today there are hints that the old economic armor is starting to chip and peel as fresh, new policies come into the picture. Most notably, *perestroika* and *glasnost* in the Soviet Union, the economic reforms in China and Eastern Europe, and the wave of economic restructuring as the US and most other industrial countries and developing countries adjust to the new Era of Global Interdependence.

International Cooperation

Nations in today's world become unmanageable when they ignore variables outside their borders. Such variables lie beyond the control of any single nation, and so every nation must adjust its policies and restructure its social systems accordingly.

Table 1

Country Futures Indicators
(Beyond GNP)

Elements of a reformulated GNP to correct errors and provide more information:

Purchasing power parity: corrects for currency fluctuation.

Income distribution: is the poverty gap widening or narrowing?

Community-based accounting: to complement current enterprise-based accounting.

Informal and household sector production: measures productive hours worked (paid and unpaid)

Deduction of social and environmental costs: a "net" accounting which helps avoid double-counting.

Account for depletion of nonrenewable resources

Energy input/GDP ratio: measure of energy efficiency and recycling.

Military/civilian budget ratio: effectiveness of government-diplomatic skills.

Capital asset accounts: for built infrastructure and public resources.

Complementary indicators of progress toward societal goals:

Education: literacy levels, school dropout and repetition rates.

Health: infant mortality, low birth weight, weight-height-age ratios.

Nutrition

Basic service: water, sanitation, telephones, electrification, etc.

Shelter

Child development

Political participation and democratic process

Status of minority and ethnic populations and women

Air and water quality and environmental pollution levels: air pollution in urban areas.

Environmental resource depletion: hectares of land, forests lost annually.

Biodiversity and species loss

Cultural and recreational resources

Copyright © 1988 by Hazel Henderson

At the heart of the problem is the traditional I-Win/You-Lose idea. Today, that is being quickly replaced by a Win/Win game in which all the players are cooperative and each player aims at a finish that will satisfy all players. In the new global game nobody wins unless everybody wins. When some individuals or groups or nations act selfishly, everyone comes out a little worse off. In a crowded football stadium, for example, when spectators insist on standing to see better, other people are forced to stand up as well. Before long no one has a better view but everyone is less comfortable.

The old win/lose game of intense competition between the US and USSR to build strong militaries has brought economic distress to both countries. While the US has become the world's deepest debtor nation, the Soviets have been forced to undergo an economic revolution to restructure their society.

Win/win rules are vital in managing the global commons, which has grown to include the atmosphere, the oceans, space, and the electromagnetic spectrum. As information and money begin to flow more smoothly and interchangeably around the world, the global economy itself has become a commons.

So the time has come to update the old maps that have been guiding our nations' political and economic policies. Each country has to become more world-minded and cooperative. For a nation to give up some of its sovereignty is far less risky than trying to go it alone. Still, economic advisors today tell their political leaders the same old story: be competitive. It is time for all governments to help retrain their economic advisors or replace them with systems theorists studying change, futurists, psychologists, engineers, anthropologists, scientists, ecologists, and other interdisciplinary advisors.

Today the world is being transformed by a new process—mutually assured development. While the mutually assured destructive policies of the superpowers have brought the US and USSR to the verge of economic ruin, fresh new cooperative policies are being launched by Japan, China, India and the newly industrializing countries of the South. Japan's consumer goods based economy accounts for about one-fourth of all the world's capital. Japanese officials are formulating plans to use much of their nation's profits to help developing countries. Thus the agenda of redefining "development" in sustainable terms is now urgent.

A Case for Competition

So far this chapter may have implied that cooperation is good, competition is bad, which is certainly not the case. There is obviously a place in the world for both, and not only in societies. The inner workings of ecosystems can be highly competitive with animals fighting or fleeing to survive, while the inner workings of organisms like the human body are mostly cooperative—specialized cells working together. Ecosystems, like societies, are continually balancing both strategies in a process called "symbiosis." But it is sometimes necessary when you have an *un*balanced situation like today's world economy, to come out strongly emphasizing the neglected portion—cooperation—so as to restore the vital balance.

Market theory today focuses almost exclusively on the competitive half. Through most of history our social systems have grown larger, from tribes and city-states to the nation-states of today. Now we are moving to the global level, and at that point markets turn into a "commons" area, the cooperative half. The rules of the game turn completely around. Before, you needed to compete as a nation to survive. Now if you don't cooperate, you

---

Trust

Reversing today's problems will require trust, the binding substance of every social system. Trust within families and among them, within nations and among them.

Many individuals have emotional scars and imbalances from childhood that act as a barrier of mistrust with others—family, friends, people at work, strangers. Healing one's life must include efforts to unravel these psychological quirks and build trust between oneself and others.

Similarly, many nations, religions and other large groups have deep-seated cultural scars and imbalances that present a barrier between those groups and their ability to trust other groups, resulting in a chronic mistrust of other cultures. Among the prominent international institutions today in need of major changes is economic theory which promotes mistrust and overconsumption.

Achieving a healthy planet will involve coming to grips with these deep-seated cultural quirks, melting away the barriers and fostering international trust.

—MHM

could destroy each other along with the Natural elements of this planet on which we all depend.

Governments that cling stubbornly to their sovereignty risk economic collapse. Global cooperation and economic interdependence are an inevitable reality, and there are two ways to get there. We can either learn the hard way, with a global depression, or we can formulate a new set of values and goals to run the new global playing field.

Before the realities of the industrial age based on competition give way and balance is restored with the much older, stabler systems of Nature and common interests, the societies of the world will shift toward sustainable forms of development and will restore older human values and cultural values that have been set aside throughout much of this century. Only then will the global economy become more stable.

A peaceful society is one that is based on renewable resources, sustainable forms of production and consumption, and a sense of justice and fairness in sharing with a reasonable amount of equity. These kinds of societies are needed if we are to create a peaceful world.

Already the growing number of cooperative areas is encouraging:

• With the world postal system you can mail a letter from anywhere in the world with the reasonable assurance that it will get to its destination. The world postal system is the result of some very sensible agreements among all countries. It is certainly not dictating its policies on anyone but provides a valuable service—worldwide communication—which no single nation can achieve by itself.

• And there is the world weather-tracking service. A complicated network of satellites and high-technology ground stations provide us here on Earth with an almost first hand look at the weather patterns going on around the face of the globe. Accurate weather forecasts have become a routine matter.

• There is the system of global air transport. If you wish to fly anywhere in the world, you can purchase a similar ticket wherever you happen to be, and the agents with all the computers at their disposal can link you up with other airlines. You know that the flights will be reasonably safe, and while standards for traffic controllers are reliable, airports will be the same.

A world of sustainable development is built upon such cooperative strategies as these. The planet itself, Gaia, has become one vast, interdependent system composed of social systems, ecosystems and other living systems that are best managed cooperatively in a win-win setting. If we fail to approach our current situation in that manner, we will charge like lemmings to extinction. Once we can restore the solid values and visions of many generations and we can adapt them to today's world of sustainable, life-enhancing technologies, we will at last have found true paths toward a healthy planet.

As concerned citizens are linking up around the world, a planetary awareness is taking shape that includes ecological sanity, social justice, and sustainable development. We can all help build the emerging "win-win world."

Notes

Some of the views and ideas for this chapter were found in articles by or interviews of Hazel Henderson which were published in:
- *The Futurist* (March-April 1988), a publication of the World Future Society
- *Plowshare Press* (Autumn 1987)
- *Calypso Log* (December 1986), a publication of the Cousteau Society
- *New Age Journal* (March 1984)
    Reprinted with permission from the World Future Society and the Cousteau Society. *New Age Journal* kindly gives rights back to the author a year after publication. *Plowshare Press* could not be reached by phone or letter.
    More of the author's views can be found in more than 200 journal articles, two books, and her contributions to six anthologies.

Books:

The Politics of the Solar Age: Alternatives to Economics, Doubleday, New York 1981; New Edition: Knowledge Systems Inc., Indianapolis, IN 1988

Creating Alternative Futures: The End of Economics, G.P. Putnam, New York 1978

Anthologies:

Redefining Wealth and Progress, The Caracas Report on Alternative Development Indicators, Knowledge Systems Inc., Indianapolis 1988

Gaia: A Way of Knowing, Political Implications of the New Biology, Ed: William Irwin Thompson, Lindisfarne Press, Hudson, NY 1987

What I Have Learned: Thinking About the Future Then and Now, Eds: Michael Marien and Lane Jennings, Greenwood Press, New York 1987

The Global Economy: Today, Tomorrow and the Transition, Ed: Howard Didsbury Jr., World Future Society, Washington, DC 1985

Learning Tomorrows, Commentaries on the Future of Education, Ed: Peter H. Wagschal, Praeger, New York 1979

Relating Work and Education, Current Issues in Higher Education, Ed: Dyckman W. Vermilye, Jossey-Bass, San Francisco 1977

America in Crisis, Contemporary Political Dilemmas, Eds: Raymond Lee and Dorothy Palmer, Winthrop, Cambridge 1972

Chapter Ten:
Global Healing
Through Global Education

by Dr. Robert Muller

His background. During 38 years of service to the UN, held many positions, including Assistant to three Secretaries-General, and earned many fond nicknames, among them "The UN Prophet" and "the first 21st-century man." More recently, as Chancellor of the UN University for Peace, he has been called "The Father of Global Education." Retired in 1986, he is becoming one of the most important and sought-after peacemakers of our time, admired for his unconditional love of planet and unwillingness to accept anything less than a happy future for humanity. Received the 1989 UNESCO Peace Education Prize. As author and lecturer, received numerous awards for global service and humanism. Wherever in the world there are initiatives, projects and conferences for peace and international development, chances are the name of Robert Muller will come up.

His chapter. The biggest single step toward international security and world peace will be the adoption by all schools of a global curriculum that will teach children love and respect for their planet, their friends, families and, most of all, themselves. Mr. Muller and his friends and associates around the world are creating such a curriculum. This chapter explains the need for the global curriculum and briefly outlines a framework recommended by the author.

Wrong education is the principal cause of political disorder on this planet; people with limited vision can only produce limited solutions.

Global Healing Through Global Education

by Robert Muller

The world is my country; to do good is my religion.
—Thomas Paine

One out of four people on the planet are illiterate; they cannot read or write their own name. Healing the world must begin with a new form of education that can teach children not only an understanding of their surroundings but also a love and respect for the planet and for other people. That was not possible 50 years ago but it is today, thanks in large part to the United Nations.

The Role of the United Nations

The United Nations Organization is often dismissed as lofty, unrealistic and ineffective in achieving its goals of peace and kinship. In fact it has helped to shape the ethics and evolution of humanity while amassing an incredible amount of knowledge during the past 40 years on subjects from the infinitely small, such as atoms and cells, to the infinitely large—knowledge of our globe and its exact position in relation to the countless stars and galaxies in the universe—the condition of our biosphere, and the seas, the oceans and the land masses. Most of this information has been gathered into the UN through its 32 specialized agencies and global programs. As a result we can educate our children in a way that children have never been educated before about our miraculously rich, life-teeming planet circling in the vast universe.

The UN may not provide immediate solutions to world crises, but over an extended period the problems are cleared up. You begin to notice, for example, that the actions of nations are damaging the seas and oceans. You call a world conference, a law-of-the-sea treaty is signed and governments immediately begin to wake up. As years pass, the rate of deterioration begins to diminish.

Or you see the planet endangered by spreading poverty and pollution. You appoint a commission to come up with solutions, and after three years of exhaustive public hearings and meetings with peasants, Presidents and other people of all continents, the commission presents the Brundtland Report, showing what it will take to build a healthy planet. Within a year the report is being scrutinized by the UN, regional organizations, national governments, NGOs and major corporations, many of whom start adjusting their policies and priorities accordingly. Universities build graduate courses around it. Schools around the globe incorporate it into their curricula.

The UN is indeed causing immense, positive changes in the world, and rather quickly. But the truly grand changes will come more slowly as the findings of the UN are assimilated into children's minds through the classroom, and the children grow into responsible, world-minded adults.

Knowing our World

If our globe could speak, it would say to us: "You make me laugh, you humans. I have been twirling around for four and a half billion years. I have seen many upheavals in my flesh; I have seen continents disappear, seas change place, mountains surge, ice covers come and go, an atmosphere be born, vegetation arise, life develop, species evolve and disappear. You came into being only two or three million years ago. I have seen you crawl in utter ignorance for most of this time. Only a few hundred years ago did you at long last discover that I was round and older than just a few thousand years. I have been observing you, and I must say, you will go nowhere if you do not remember that I will be around for several billion years more, that my body will be shaken by many more climatic changes, that for your maximum enjoyment and survival you must treat and manage me with care. After your cave age, after your tribal age, after your feudal age, after your national age, you have at long last entered my age: the global age. As you come into my age you must come as caretakers or you may not last long here."

An important recent view has been to see the entire history of our planet reduced to the span of one day: the birth of the human race occurs only five minutes before midnight and the industrial civilization only at the first stroke of the clock at 12. Another view is to see that we have still two long days before us and that this first stroke of midnight is in reality the first strike of the global age.

Global education must prepare our children for the coming age of interdependence, prosperity, and friendly, loving, happy people—the planetary age heralded by the great prophets. Humanity has passed through many great ages. The truly great period of human fulfillment on our planet is now to begin.

That becomes evident when we see what has been happening during the last 40 years. The recent acceleration of industry, science and technology has had far-reaching effects on three aspects of our lives. First is the incredible improvement of living conditions on our planet. While regrettable discrepancies keep the poorer parts at a lower level of consumption than that of the US and the rest of the West, even in the poorer parts of the world the quantity of goods placed at the disposal of the individual is increasing.

The second effect is the well-documented, accelerated growth of the human race. We doubled from 2.5 billion in 1951 to 5 billion in 1987. Statistics published by the UN and its agencies show that the world data base has doubled or tripled during the past 20 years.

The third effect is a network of global interdependencies among societies which is growing more and more dense at an accelerating rate. Thousands of planes, ships and trains are on the move constantly. Airports and seaports cannot keep up with the growing traffic. These interdependencies have forced governments and individuals into a new type of collective thinking about our globe.

Quality Education in a Global Sense

For true planetary healing, it is time now to reform the curriculum to give children an honest, objective view of our wonderful world and ourselves—our exact place in space and time. And the means of moving from a troubled past to a peaceful future.

Wrong education is the principal cause of the political disorder on this planet. People with a limited vision can only produce limited solutions. We need hosts of people with a world vision. Children of today and of the past are taught that the groups into which they are born are superior to the totality. A nation or culture is shown to be greater than the sum of its parts. Greater than humanity. Their language more important than clear worldwide communication. A national ideology superior to global ideas. A religious ritual more valuable than universal spirituality. There's nothing wrong with pride in one's group, but the time has come for everyone to reserve a place at the top of their list of loves and devotions for the most important membership of all— our membership to humanity and the world. Nothing is more important today than teaching children the right attitude toward life, peace and progress. The idea that the world is one, humanity is one, and the individual and humanity are greater realities than any nation.

My beloved master Secretary-General U Thant often told me, "Robert, our own generation will not achieve world peace. For that we need a new generation properly educated about the world, the human family and the supreme worth of the individual person."

He saw an urgent need, in a world divided by national interests, for an education which would teach each human being to give precedence to life, to the world and to humanity, reconciling citizenship with human allegiance, efficiency with humanism, and national objectives with world objectives. A journalist once asked him what in his view was the most important single obstacle to world peace. He answered that it was the principle "my country, right or wrong."

U Thant was probably the greatest teacher of my life. He had been a teacher in his country, Burma, before being elected to the highest office in the United Nations. In one of his farewell speeches upon leaving the UN (a speech to planetary citizens) he said:

> I believe that an ideal man or woman is endowed with four virtues, four qualities—physical, mental, moral and spiritual qualities. I attach importance to all of them, but I would attach greater importance to the mental or intellectual over the physical qualities. Still I would rate moral qualities higher than intellectual qualities. Still more, I would rate spiritual qualities the highest. It is far from my intention to downgrade or denigrate the physical and intellectual aspects of life. I am in no sense an anti-intellectual, but the stress of education in the schools of the highly developed societies is primarily on the development of the intellect or on physical excellence, without taking into account the moral and spiritual aspects

of life, which I consider far more important than the physical and intellectual aspects. That is why I have tried to develop, without perfection alas, those moral virtues and spiritual qualities like modesty, humility, love, compassion, the philosophy of live and let live, the desire to understand the other person's point of view, which constitute the keys to all great religions.

U Thant believed that peace on earth could be achieved only through proper education of the younger generations and that spirituality deserved the highest place in such education. May

---

What Is Spirituality?

We live in two worlds, one being the familiar world of material things that we see, hear, feel, taste and smell. We also live part of our lives in the spirit world. Spirituality is the practice of linking to the spirit world in our day-to-day, waking lives. While the body and mind are our vehicles for the physical world, the heart is our link to the spirit world. Well-aged, indigenous cultures foster a link between the people and the spirit world through customs, beliefs and rituals which kindle the heart. With the modernization of western society this link has been crimped and constricted so that about the only occasions our spirit or self communes with other spirits is when we are unconscious (in dreams or sleep) and when we die. We are consciously oblivious to the spirit world. A healthy link can gradually be restored by such practices as meditation and deep prayer.

Spirituality is not the same as religion. A religion is an institution and set of practices which may or may not encourage its members to become spritual beings. Indeed, some religious organizations have been said to sustain their power by keeping their members in spiritual darkness. The organization remains strong by keeping its members spiritually weak and dependent upon the religious leadership.

The world is calling out now for all individuals to kindle their hearts and become spiritual beings as well as physical and mental beings. Individuals who link to the spirit world through meditation, deep prayer and other such means eventually begin to commune with nonmaterial beings, which have been called angels, spirits, souls, chindi, beings of the light and other such names.

The wonderful feelings and the tremendous unspoken insights derived from such encounters are documented in many books, both religious and secular, current and ancient. If you can learn how to bring your consciousness into your heart while meditating, you will gradually develop an intimate link with the spirit world. I'm sure there are other methods, but I can vouch for this one.

—MHM

the current concern for proper global education allow for spirituality, love and compassion to be given generous room in all the world's educational systems. It is in our highest interest to do so, if we want to stem war, violence, crime and unhappiness. May all educators heed these wise words of U Thant, one of the first global teachers and spiritual masters of the nascent world community:

> The law of love and compassion for all living creatures is again a doctrine to which we are all too ready to pay lip service. However, if it is to become a reality, it requires a process of education, a veritable mental renaissance. Once it has become a reality, national as well as international problems will fall into perspective and become easier to solve. Wars and conflicts, too, will then become a thing of the past, because wars begin in our minds, and in our minds love and compassion would have built the defenses of peace.

Teachers of today deserve our utmost support in instilling such ideas in their students. Many teachers and educational theorists are advancing quite nicely along these lines, among them Gloria Crook, Andy LePage, and Betty Reardon.

Gloria Crook operates a school in Arlington, Texas, where the children are taught about their place in the universe in the simplest way: they are asked to answer the following question, describe the listed items, and draw at the end a picture of their home. Children who have done this exercise develop a keen sense of their place in the world and get a healthy overall perspective on life.

WHERE ARE WE?
- Universe:
- Galaxy:
- Sun System:
- Planet:
- Hemisphere:
- Continent:
- Country:
- State or Province:
- City:
- Street:
- Name:

Andy LePage, having gone through seminary and serving as a teacher, a teacher trainer and a therapist, analyzes the pitfalls of modern education and describes some alternatives in his book, *Transforming Education*. Here are excerpts:

> According to a recent report, money is the number one concern of US school superintendents. Other worries include instructional programs, teacher training programs, improving test scores, administrators' training, and the recruitment of good teachers. One could conclude from this poll that several million dollars and a few well placed programs would solve the difficulties in education. This is not so.
>
> The problems in education originate in the roots of the soil of social change centuries old. Pruning the tree when the soil is polluted and the roots are dying, will not result in the new growth of buds.
>
> Schools are giving specific content, but that content does not really help students develop self-confidence, become self-responsible, instruct them in caring for property, or help them in their character development . . . knowledge which is seemingly supposed to come about by some process of osmosis. Somehow, students are expected to pick up these needed qualities from the air, and begin enriching society.
>
> A curriculum for today's world must be inclusive, life relevant, practical, and teach stewardship—responsibility—for the earth. We are stewards of the earth. It is our home, it contains our support system. Our educational curriculum must address it. We have to know how to live in balance with its ecology so we can offer it whole and intact to our children, and their children.
>
> An internship should be designed to give students experience in social change. Sixth to eighth graders could be apprentice workers while high school students could take on leadership and world roles. They could work in such areas as:
> - health care for senior citizens
> - neighborhood cultural events such as mime, storytelling, music, dance, juggling, poetry, art and so on
> - housing rehabilitation in blighted areas
> - cooperative gardening and farm stand
> - handyperson program for fixing things and learning such skills as negotiation and price-setting
> - daycare and parenting center

- assessing neighborhood needs for outreach programs to teach people of all ages in all sorts of courses, including neighborhood organizing and empowerment, assertiveness, self-esteem, parenting, beginning and ending relationships, and compassion.

Betty Reardon is director of Peace Education at Columbia University Teachers College and former member of the Council of the University for Peace, Costa Rica. Her peace curriculum advocates that in the first place educators teach the experience developed by the UN, a wealth of experience that should not be ignored. This should be followed by the world core curriculum (outlined below), which offers the largest framework available within which peace education can unfold. Finally, peace education should deal with the specific problem areas of peace—conflict resolution, disarmament, human rights, poverty, etc. This is the approach Betty Reardon takes in her book, *Comprehensive Peace Education—Educating for Global Responsibility*. It is truly a book for everyone.

The knowledge and experience provided by such world-minded educators as Betty Reardon, Andy LePage and Gloria Crook will shape our children into responsible citizens of our societies and our planet.

A World Core Curriculum

I believe the ideal framework for global education would be all-inclusive, revolving around four basic oceans of information: 1) our planet and its place in the universe, 2) the human family, 3) our place in time, and 4) individual life.

Our planetary home and place in the universe. First, my curriculum would deal with planet Earth. Humanity has been able, of late, to produce a magnificent picture of our planet and of its place in the universe. From the infinitely large to the infinitely small, everything fits today in a very simple and clear pattern. Most of this information is used today in the United Nations.

The framework allows us to present our planetary and universal knowledge to all people and particularly to children in a simple, beautiful way. They wish to be told about their correct place in the universe. The Greeks' and Pascal's genial view of the infinitely large and the infinitely small has been filled in by science and provides the framework for much of today's world cooperation and daily lives of people. We can now give children a breathtaking view of the beauty and teeming, endless richness of our world as has never been possible before. It should make students glad to be alive and to be human.

This knowledge gives the teachers of this world a marvelous opportunity to teach children and people a sense of participation and responsibility in the building and management of the Earth, of being artisans of our further human ascent. A new world morality and world ethics will thus evolve all along the above scale, and teachers will be able to prepare responsible citizens involved in science, genetics, physics, and scores of other professions, including a new one which is badly needed: good world management and caretaking.

The human family. There is a second segment on which humanity has also made tremendous progress of late: not only have we taken cognizance of our planet and of our place in the universe, but we have also taken stock of ourselves. This is of momentous importance for henceforth our story in the universe is basically that of ourselves and of our planet. For a proper unfolding of that story, we had to know its two main elements well: the planet and ourselves. This has been accomplished since World War II. The planetary and human inventories are now practically complete.

Our place in time. In the same way as humanity is taking cognizance of its correct place in the universe, we are now also forced to look at our correct place in time or eternity. We are forced to expand our time dimension tremendously both into the past and into the future. We must preserve the natural elements inherited from the past and necessary for our life and survival (air, water, soils, energy, animals, fauna, flora, genetic materials). We also want to preserve our cultural heritage, the landmarks of our own social evolution and history in order to see the unfolding and magnitude of our cosmic journey. At the same time, we must think and plan far ahead into the future in order to hand over to coming generations a well preserved and better managed planet in the universe. What does this mean for a world curriculum? It means that we must add a time dimension to the above layers, each of which has a past, present and future.

The miracle and fulfillment of individual life. It has become increasingly clear that in this vast evolutionary quantum change the individual remains the alpha and the omega of all our efforts. Individual human life is the highest form of universal consciousness on our planet. Institutions, concepts, factories, systems, states, ideologies, theories have no consciousness. They are all servants, instruments, means for better lives and the increase of individual human consciousness.

We are faced today with the full-fledged centrality, dignity, miracle, sanctity or divinity of individual human life, irrespective of race, sex, status, age, nation, physical or mental capacity.

An immense global task and responsibility thus behooves all teachers and educators of this planet. It is no less than to contribute to the survival and good management of our planetary home and species, to our further common ascent into a universal, interdependent, peaceful civilization, while ensuring the knowledge, skills and fulfillment of all beings prepared for life by the Earth's schools.

Notes

Some of the views and ideas for this chapter were found in the following books by Robert Muller:

- *A Planet of Hope*, Amity House Inc., Rockport, 1985
- *Most of All They Taught Me Happiness*, World Happiness and Cooperation, Ardsley on Hudson, 1989
- *New Genesis*, World Happiness and Cooperation, Ardsley on Hudson, 1989
- *What War Taught Me About Peace*, Doubleday, New York, 1985
- *The World Core Curriculum*, Robert Muller School, Arlington (Texas)

Chapter Eleven:
Guidelines for
New Citizen Diplomats

by John W. McDonald

His background. President of the Iowa Peace Institute after 40 years of diplomatic service with the US government. Teaches, advises and lectures at numerous US institutes and universities. Author of many articles and books on negotiation, conflict resolution, aging, the disabled, water and sanitation, and various UN issues. Has spent 20 years in Western Europe and the Middle East and has worked on UN social and economic issues for 16 years. Has visited more than 75 countries on five continents. Doctorate of Law (University of Illinois).

His chapter. If undertaken properly, citizen diplomacy can play an invaluable role in international peace making, easing anger, tension and fear while circumventing the more formal and rigid official diplomatic channels. But mishandled, it can do just the opposite. The author offers some important guidelines for citizen diplomacy which make it clear that knowledge and good human skills are vital along with a desire to help.

"Official diplomacy" is seen as ignoring or rejecting ideas that responsible private citizens believe should at least be explored—hence the citizen diplomat.

Guidelines for New Citizen Diplomats

by John W. McDonald

Track Two diplomacy, commonly called "citizen diplomacy," is a form of conflict resolution that is non-governmental, informal and unofficial. It is interaction between private citizens, or groups of people within a country or from different countries, who are outside the formal governmental power structure. Persons involved in Track Two efforts have as their objective the reduction or resolution of conflict, within a country or between countries, by lowering the anger, tension or fear that exists, by facilitating improved communications and by helping to bring about a better understanding of each other's point of view.

Track One diplomacy, on the other hand, is government-to-government, formal, sometimes even rigid, official interaction between instructed representatives of sovereign states. Track Two diplomacy should be viewed quite positively by Track One diplomats as a major tool in the world's search for peace and the reduction of conflict because it is more flexible, less structured, more innovative (. . . and more deniable in the event it does not work).

Unfortunately, this positive view of Track Two diplomacy is not the case. Track One usually ignores Track Two completely or denigrates its efforts as being ineffective and a waste of Track One's time. This is unfortunate because much good could emerge from planned interactions between Tracks One and Two. Track One should recognize that Track Two is not designed or intended to supplant Track One, so no threat exists. In addition every Track Two diplomat recognizes that if they are truly effective in doing their job and succeed in reducing fear and anger between the parties, this will help Track One get to the negotiating table and begin to formally resolve their differences.

I do believe one of the principal reasons that interest in Track Two in the United States has increased so dramatically in the past few years, with particular focus on US-Soviet, Central American, South African and Northern Ireland problems, is that Track One is seen as ignoring or rejecting ideas that responsible private citizens believe should at least be explored by the government. These same citizens have often turned to Track Two out of a sense of frustration, believing that doing something is better than doing nothing.

One excellent example of this frustration has been the work done by the Natural Resources Defense Council (NRDC). This private citizen's group was disappointed at the US government's refusal to join a nuclear testing moratorium begun by the Soviets in August, 1985, because the US government said the ban could not be verified. NRDC actually negotiated and signed an agreement with the Soviets in May, 1986, permitting on-site verification in the Soviet Union. US and Soviet scientists agreed that three seismic stations would be set up within 120 miles of the main Soviet nuclear testing site and would be staffed jointly by US and Soviet scientists.

This Track Two action was accomplished by private US scientists working with private Soviet scientists. Their actions have now pushed the US government into a Track One agreement with the Soviet government along the lines of the Track Two understanding.

My recognition of the need for some voluntary but informative guidelines came about in the following manner.

In June, 1986, I chaired a panel on Track Two Diplomacy at the Denver, Colorado, meeting of the National Conference on Peacemaking and Conflict Resolution. One of my panelists was Katherine Kennedy, from Melrose, MA, who spoke with great feeling and insight based on her long experience as a Track Two citizen diplomat involved in the Northern Ireland dispute. A number of people came up to her after the panel to ask questions and, by the end of the conference, Katherine told me that some thirty people asked her how to get involved in Northern Ireland. It turned out that five or six of this group, all complete novices, actually turned up in Northern Ireland that summer. Katherine became quite upset—she was worried about their impact on Northern Ireland's problems, because of their inexperience and also about their physical safety—being of good heart was not nearly enough! On her return from Northern Ireland that fall, we agreed that something had to be done to try to bring about a greater understanding of the Track Two process.

On December 4, 1986, I invited 27 people to the State Department's Center for the Study of Foreign Affairs, for a one day workshop on "Track Two Diplomacy: Its Limitations and Opportunities." The attendees had a copy of my paper entitled "Guidelines for Newcomers to Track Two Diplomacy" and we spent the day discussing the issues raised and critiquing my draft paper.

In August of 1987, I re-wrote the earlier draft completely and recirculated it to the 27 persons who had been invited to attend the December meeting.

Track Two diplomacy, defined here as reducing ethnic or sectarian conflict, is designed specifically to de-escalate international conflict. The guidelines for newcomers to the field of Track Two are also intended to be used in order to understand how private citizens can make a more effective impact on a particular conflict and bring about some reduction or de-escalation of tension and fear.

I wish to thank the participants in this exercise for their insights and to thank Katherine for pushing me to do something about this problem. The following guidelines are mine alone, however, and I take full responsibility for the language and content. My real hope is that they will be read—and followed— by newcomers to the field.

Guidelines for Newcomers to Track Two Diplomacy

These guidelines are designed to help those individuals who are interested in seriously exploring the possibility of becoming involved in third party facilitation of ethnic or sectarian conflict. The guidelines are divided into four phases, each building on the previous phase, and should not be viewed as negative, oppressive or restrictive. They are designed to focus the newcomer's attention on the serious nature of the subject. Third party facilitation is an extraordinarily sensitive, sometimes life-threatening issue, and requires extensive knowledge of the process. Being a US citizen, I list these guidelines with other US citizens in mind, though they can probably be applied to any nationality.

Phase One: Exploring Your Subject and Yourself

If you are serious about this form of Track Two diplomacy you must become knowledgeable about the subject. The field is relatively new, however, and there are only a handful of books on the market dealing with citizen diplomacy. Become familiar with them and even discuss your interests with some of the authors, if possible. Inform yourself about the role of a facilitator and how that differs from an arbitrator, a mediator or a Track One diplomat. Study intercultural communication and recognize that we Americans have our own cultural biases. Be aware of what is possible and what is not possible to achieve in this general field. Know the difference between conflict management and conflict resolution and understand "win-win" versus "win-lose", as well as the value of consensus. Become familiar with the literature on the art and science of negotiation, both at the national and the international level.

Once you are familiar with the literature, take a look at yourself. Do you have some of the attributes that make a good facilitator?

Compassion. Compassion, sympathy, enthusiasm, and the desire to want to help your fellow citizens is fine, in fact necessary, but it is not nearly enough.

Patience. Americans are a very impatient people. They should recognize that and not try to impose their sense of time or schedule on an on-going process.

Humility. Modesty and humility do not come easy to Americans, who often think they have all the answers to the world's problems. We have to recognize that we can learn from other nationalities.

Good Faith. Honesty, integrity and good faith are essential elements in trying to establish a trust relationship with all of the parties involved. This takes time to achieve.

Personal Interests. Be careful of your own ego. Do not seek to advance your own interests at the expense of other parties involved. A facilitator should be impartial.

Creativity. Are you a creative person? One of the strengths of Track Two diplomacy is that it encourages an innovative and unconventional approach to old problems.

Qualifications. There are no automatic credentials for entering this sophisticated field that, once met, make you a Track Two facilitator. Personal integrity, intelligence, expertise in related fields, extensive experience in cross-cultural dispute resolution and common sense will all help to build your credibility. The building of credibility is a gradual and ongoing process.

Phase Two: Analysis and Involvement

Having passed through Phase One successfully, you now have to analyze your own interests and prepare your involvement in the Track Two process. The following points must be considered:

Focus. It is more useful to focus on one conflict and develop expertise in that area than to move from conflict to conflict. Try not to overload the channels of communication, however. Be aware that the Soviet Union, Northern Ireland and South Africa are currently very popular Track Two subjects in the United States.

Communicate with Others. No matter what conflict you want to focus on, remember, many have been there before you. Find out who they are, get to know them, learn from them. Perhaps you should join ranks and work together rather than going it alone. Others can teach you a great deal.

Knowledge of the Subject. Once you have decided on the area you wish to pursue, immerse yourself in the subject. Read widely, identify the issues and the different points of view, talk to knowledgeable persons in this country and become familiar with the history, religion, culture, mores and even the language of the groups with which you will be interacting.

Develop a Plan. Carefully think through your aspirations and your potential role, and then develop a written plan identifying your goals and methods. Goals should be realistic and should be projected over a five year period.

Define the Process. Make it clear from the beginning that you are not speaking for or representing the United States Government, but that you are acting on your own or as a part of a non-governmental group or institution.

Institutional Support. You should try to obtain some form of institutional support. Having the backing of a University or Foundation, or a non-governmental organization, will increase considerably your credibility and effectiveness. Free agents or individuals are discouraged by all parties.

Equality. Experience has shown that interaction among people of equal status is often more effective than when the disparities are too great. This will also make access and credibility easier.

Agenda for Solutions. A newcomer's agenda for a "solution" probably has been thought of and rejected years ago. Do not try to impose your solutions on their problems, but try to work with them to take small steps which may lead to their solution.

Commitment. Any conflict you may become involved in will probably have been going on for years or decades, if not for hundreds of years. Outsiders are often not welcome, and certainly

---

The Global Brain and the Human Heart

Major changes are underway as information begins to spread freely around the globe. Now is a good time to start assembling a global data base — a computerized encyclopedia of all facts and figures known by humanity. Someone wishing to know the size and function of a sheep's intestine or the location of the world's largest bridge or the names of the first cosmonauts to spend more than a month in space, could simply turn on a computer terminal, link into a global information network, perform a quick search, and print out the desired information. Literally, all the world's knowledge would be at our fingertips.

Currently there exist numerous nationwide and international data-bases that computer users can subscribe to and link to over phone lines, but most of these networks deal with information that is specialized or otherwise limited in scope. None approach the massive scope of a well-managed, comprehensive, global, electronic encyclopedia that our descendants will need next century to sustain a healthy, complex world. A global brain of this type could provide a foundation for global education and a pure world democracy managed by five billion well-versed individuals.

Meanwhile it is vital that valuable ideas, feelings and skills possessed by one culture be encouraged to spread into other cultures and around the globe, however possible, whether electronically, in printed materials, or by face-to-face meetings. Interpersonal encounters seem to be the most meaningful and lasting method of information interchange, as they can touch the hearts of everyone involved.

—MHM

newcomers who arrive, wave the magic wand of their "solution" and then depart, are even less welcome. Your presence must be seen as a commitment, which will take time, human resources, money and patience. There are no quick, easy solutions left.

Timing. The timing of your initial entrance onto the scene is most important and should be carefully considered and coordinated with others who are operating in your subject area.

Phase Three: Follow-Through

An understanding of the principles as well as the ethical standards defined in Phase Two are essential to your success. Now that you have started down the facilitator's challenging path, what are some of the specifics that you should be aware of, if you do not want to abort your efforts early in the process?

Contacts. Well before you leave the United States, contacts must have been made with the parties concerned. They must provide you with some signal that they agree to your involvement and give you an indication as to the timing of your arrival. Actually, the development of a joint venture, where all parties have equal status, will give the project more credibility.

Personal Safety. It is recommended that on arrival in a country you advise the US Embassy of your presence and the length of your stay. You might even call on the Embassy Political Officer for a briefing on the current situation. This should not be viewed as an infringement upon your privacy or a constraint on your freedom of movement, but rather as a safety precaution, designed to protect your person.

Promises-Promises. Do not raise unjustified hopes in the hearts and minds of the participants about rosy conclusions to be reached, monies forthcoming, projects to be launched, etc. False promises and raised expectations are far worse than no promises at all.

Confidentiality. Off-the-record interactions are absolutely essential to success. This means no press releases, press conferences, speeches, articles, books or media coverage about your role. Even if some modest success is achieved, it can be nullified immediately by premature, unilateral publicity. Confidentiality, by all parties, is critical to success. If progress is made, at some appropriate point a joint communique can be negotiated and released by all parties simultaneously. Unilateral publicity, by whatever party, is always destructive.

Phase Four: Disengagement and Aftermath

Now that you have completed a segment of your long-range goal, you must realize that no ethnic or sectarian conflict will ever be "resolved" by one event in the scheme of things. What are your next concerns?

Re-entry Problems. A Track Two practitioner must be particularly sensitive to what is known as the "re-entry" problem. This problem occurs after the involved parties have left their homelands to participate in Track Two meetings designed to foster greater understanding and reduce fear and tension, and then are ready to return to their constituencies and homes after the interaction is over. This return or "re-entry" into what could be a hostile environment, can be dangerous to the participants and must be carefully discussed in advance and the re-entry well managed to insure the minimum of danger to the returnees.

Handling Success. If your actions, over time, bring about some forward movement, some progress or small success in the conflict you are working with, you should, as appropriate, inform your government. You should not view this suggestion as a restraint on your efforts. The government representative you contact, either in-country or in Washington, D.C., may in fact be in a position to provide you with information or be of other help to you.

Costs. Track Two facilitators should operate on a pro-bono basis at no cost to the participants. There should be no conflict of interest between the facilitator and the other parties.

Track One - Track Two Relationship. The interrelationship between the two tracks can be a sensitive one. Track Two facilitators do not want to feel pressured or unduly constrained just because they happen to be exploring a policy that Track One opposes. Track One, on the other hand, likes to be kept informed about what is going on. Track Two facilitators must recognize, on their part, that if their initiative is successful, Track Two will probably have to merge with Track One. It is governments, after all, who are responsible for negotiating, signing and ratifying treaties and other formal documents that may be needed to seal a successful Track Two initiative.

Communication is becoming increasingly fluid among countries and cultures as we move into the new century. The many differences that have divided us in the past will continue to create some friction. If we can all learn a few basic guidelines for citizen diplomacy, we can minimize the friction.

Chapter Twelve:
The Common Heritage of Humankind

by Keith D. Suter

His background. Former director, Trinity Peace Research Institute. Independent Christian scholar. Born and educated in England, then earned a Ph.D. in The International Law of Guerilla Warfare in 1976 in Australia, where he remained to become one of the country's best-known peace activists. Former head of the UN Association of Australia. Author of seven books and numerous articles. Travels around the world for first-hand view of wars and conflicts. Chairman and member of various national and international peace-related organizations and conferences.

His chapter. The common heritage principle—the idea that some parts of the world should be internationalized, or placed beyond the limits of national jurisdictions—is now well established in international politics, but it is applied only to such uninhabited areas as the seabed, the moon and space. The author explains why it is time to broaden the scope of common heritage to include certain inhabited areas crucial to our future, such as rainforests, topsoil and the atmosphere.

Global priority setting . . .
suggests that all of humankind is
one and that it should be
interested in its long-term
survival.

The Common Heritage of Humankind

by Keith D. Suter

We are living on the hinge of history. One era is dying and another is being born. The 1970s-1990s represent the transition period. As of 1990, we are still not in a position to perceive fully what form the new era will take.

International lawyers take AD 1648 as the beginning of the modern international law era. Historians may dispute the precision of the date (which is derived from the ending of a major war in Europe), but clearly about four centuries ago the European continent made a dramatic transition from people owing their loyalty to tribes and clans, to seeing themselves as citizens of nation-states. This change coincided with the industrial revolution, with its emphasis on the division of labor, machines, factories and need for raw materials and markets for finished products.

Competition

A common feature in the rise of both the nation-state and the industrialized nation is competition: for territory, wealth, markets, and raw materials. Competition and wars have existed since the beginning of history. But the combination of factory-produced weapons and national treasuries to finance the factories and raise national armies brought a new level of destructiveness.

Competition is not inherently bad. The desire for improvement in people's lives, for example, is based on a competition between where they are and where they would like to be. However, the desire can become destructive if it becomes obsessive, such as a determination to win at all costs (such as salary increases), to ignore friends and neighbors and to seek solely self-gain.

Much the same could be said about the international level. There is nothing inherently wrong in nation-states competing against one another in the desire for economic growth. Unfortunately national governments often become obsessive about national expansion. This helps explain the current arms race, the destruction of nonrenewable resources and the lack of cooperation in helping Third World nations.

This philosophy is best illustrated in the so-called New Right. There is nothing new in economics—merely fresh variations on old themes. The New Right of the 1980s was neither New nor Right. For most of European history (AD 300 to about 1500) the Christian Church controlled economic policy and, drawing its authority from biblical instructions not to exploit the poor and weak, it laid down a detailed system of rules, such as the prohibition of usury (lending money at interest rates), regulating trading hours (to stop eager traders from selling their items before their competitors had set up their stalls) and providing clerics (clerks) to assist in the creation of fair contracts. Two centuries ago, however, Adam Smith argued that all this control stifled individual initiative, and that the fewer rules and regulations the greater scope for economic growth.

Adam Smith was right in one regard: abolishing regulations and leaving people to do their own work will result in new financial creativeness. Unfortunately, it also led to the financial chaos of the 1920s-1930s, the rise of Hitler, the Depression and World War II. During the war, western governments agreed that unregulated competition would be mutually destructive. The pendulum swung back in favor of government intervention in the economy and the creation of the welfare state.

In recent years, however, the pendulum has begun to retrace its arc. The New Right wants minimal government involvement in the national economy, and a reduction in social welfare services. It sees life as a perpetual struggle, where only the fittest will survive. Adherents of the movement as a whole are not interested in posterity. . . what has posterity done for them?

With any luck, international cooperation and sensible world policies will slow the pendulum down, and maybe stop it somewhere near center.

A Lead From the Sea

The United Nations law of the sea treaty was finalized in 1982. The United States, at the last moment, refused to sign the treaty. Other nations have signed it but are stalling on ratification of it. In due course, however, it is likely that all nations will ratify it.

An important concept in the 1982 treaty is the "common heritage of humankind." The concept has been in circulation for some years. The 1982 treaty put it specifically on the international statute books. The common heritage concept is here to stay.

The High Seas are waters outside of national control which may be used by nations but cannot be claimed by them. The sea bed beneath the High Seas, until 1945, was totally inaccessible to all nations. On November 1, 1967, Malta's representative to the UN, Arvid Pardo, warned the UN about new threats to world peace. He recalled the way in which the previously inaccessible seabed was now becoming accessible because of modern technology. He was worried about a scramble for the seabed similar to last century's scramble for Africa. He recommended that the seabed be internationalized, so as to put it beyond national appropriation, and for it to be exploited for the benefit of all humankind, and not just the minority of technologically advanced nations and transnational corporations. If the seabed could be administered smoothly, then this would be a good omen for the governance of the rest of the globe.

Dr. Pardo's proposal got a mixed reception. The western and communist developed nations were unenthusiastic, if not downright hostile, to the proposal. But the Third World nations, which constitute the majority of UN membership, liked the proposal because they could see the benefits of it. A committee was set up to examine the proposal. As its work progressed, it became clear that there would need to be a new UN Law of the Sea Conference to clarify some ambiguities in the law of the sea 1958 treaty, such as the still undecided width of the territorial sea.

The UN Committee's work climaxed with the December 17, 1970, "common heritage" resolution. Its provisions echoed, though with significant modifications, Dr. Pardo's original proposals: it called for demilitarizing the seabed, "beyond the limits of national jurisdiction," declaring it and its resources "the common heritage of mankind" and establishing for it an international regime, "including appropriate international machinery" to manage it, and "to ensure the equitable sharing by States in the benefits derived therefrom, taking into particular consideration the interests and needs of developing countries, whether landlocked or coastal." It was carried unopposed. Fourteen states abstained, including those of Eastern Europe, for whom the attractions of the call for the reservation of the area "exclusively for peaceful purposes" balanced the distaste they felt for the "common heritage" concept and the idea of establishing an international body to administer it. It was left to the Law of the Sea Conference to work out the details.

With the political climate changing quickly in Eastern Europe some major obstacles to this important law are disappearing, and things may start falling into place in the coming years.

The UN Law of the Sea Conference had its first session in New York in 1973. Its work was completed nine years later. The tragedy of the Conference's work is that the geographical area of the common heritage was eroded by an unexpected development: coastal nations insisted not only on a 12 mile territorial sea, but an exclusive economic zone (EEZ) extending for up to 188 miles beyond the territorial sea. The Maltese proposal had been eroded but not killed. The new treaty will enter into force in the 1990s.

The Moon and Outer Space

A few days before Dr. Pardo made his common heritage speech at the UN, outer space had become, in effect, the common heritage of humankind. The 1967 Treaty on Principles Governing the Activities of States in the Exploration and Use of Outer Space, including the Moon and Other Celestial Bodies, stated that the exploration and use of outer space shall be carried out for the benefit of all nations, irrespective of their degree of economic or scientific development "and shall be the province of humankind."

Outer space, including the moon and other celestial bodies, is not subject to national appropriation by claim of sovereignty, by means of use of occupation, or by any other means. Nations ratifying this treaty (and most of the world's nations have done so) agree to carry out their activities in the interest of maintaining international peace and security and promoting international cooperation and understanding.

Owing to traditional hostility between the US and USSR only small gains have come of that treaty in terms of practical cooperation.

In a better political climate, such as that now emerging, the 1967 treaty could provide an excellent basis for international cooperation. Space activities are not expensive (compared with military expenditure) and joint US-USSR activities would provide an inspiration for the entire globe.

Additionally, the concept could be applied not only to extraterrestrial resources but also to the products of space activity in general. It could be applied, for example, to information gathered by satellites, in fields such as earth resources, pollution and weather patterns.

The Antarctic

The Antarctic is governed by a 1961 treaty which demilitarized the continent and provided a basis for international scientific cooperation. The treaty was written before many of the world's nations had achieved independence and they perceive it as continuing a system similar to imperialism.

Malaysia, which is outside the Antarctic treaty, has called for a new treaty which would provide for wider international participation in the Antarctic's affairs. The Antarctic was specifically excluded from the new law of the sea and so was not covered by the common heritage concept.

The common heritage concept is not necessarily an exploitive one. It certainly began that way in the context of the seabed, but is now more about international control and administration than exploitation. Given the right political climate, the common heritage concept could be applied to the Antarctic, as in the context of some form of world park or world preserve.

The Common Heritage Concept

The seabed, the moon, outer space and (to a limited extent) the Antarctic all have in common the fact that they are beyond the scope of national control (or, in the Antarctic's case, there is no globally agreed recognition on territorial claims). An important part of the common heritage concept, then, is that each area is beyond and outside national control, that it is to be managed for the benefit of all of humankind both now and in the future, and that it should be kept for peaceful purposes.

The current concept is certainly innovative compared with New Right thinking. But can it be taken further? Is it possible to take the concept into geographical areas which are already controlled by governments?

A New Approach

The current scope of the concept's application was based on the question:
* What currently unclaimed areas may yet become subject to national claims?
* How can these unclaimed areas be preserved for the benefit of all humankind?

I would like to ask an even more ambitious question: what ecological components of the earth, whether currently claimed or unclaimed, are vital to safeguard the future of humankind? Instead of focusing on unclaimed territory, this question deals with global priority-setting. Rather than seeing the globe consisting of competing individuals and nation-states, the question suggests that all of humankind is one and that it should be interested in its long-term survival.

There are some components of the planet which are too important to all humankind to be left to the hazards of private or national control. Among these are forests, topsoil and the atmosphere.

An Enlarged Concept—Five Steps to a Secure World

"The Earth is one but the world is not," observed the 1987 Brundtland Report. "We all depend on one biosphere for sustaining our lives. Yet each community, each country, strives for survival and prosperity with little regard for its impact on others." The Brundtland Report endorsed the current Common Heritage concept. I support much of what the Brundtland Report has to say.

But I would like to go further. Consider these five steps. First, the Common Heritage concept should be based on what is required to secure the common basis of the future survival of humankind.

We need a list of what is required to ensure that the planet remains in business, irrespective of national jurisdictions.

Second, compiling the list of planetary components and doing the planetary priority-setting is a form of international goals and directions. This work should involve movements which currently concentrate on their own issues but which lack a transcending vision to bring them together, such as the ecology, peace and human rights movements. The enlarged concept of the Common Heritage could provide a rallying point.

Third, each person should see themselves as trustees of the Common Heritage. The Common Heritage can only protect humankind for as long as humankind protects the Common Heritage. Ask not what you can do for your country, but what you can do for your planet.

Doing More with Less

We see a grim picture today of an overdeveloped world trying to dump its toxic wastes in the Third World. In fact, the rich countries are doing this only after having fouled their own nests in many cases. *L'Express* newsmagazine of Paris in October 1988 listed thousands of dump sites that will have to be cleaned up in the coming years, including 20,000 in the US, 1,000 in West Germany, 380 in Denmark and 100 in France.

While it would be a mistake for the Third World to evolve in the image of the overdeveloped West, the Brundtland Report leaves little doubt that development of some type — obviously a more sustainable type — is vital. The kerosene lamp widely used throughout the Third World uses the same energy as a 100-watt light bulb but produces only one fiftieth the light, the equivalent of a 2-watt bulb, while poisoning household air.

Protecting the environment has to move to the top of our list of development considerations. The rain forests and timber stands world-wide are the lungs of the globe. They turn the carbon dioxide which we breathe out, into oxygen which we need to breathe in. Every year we destroy 77,000 square miles of rain forest, an area the size of Austria and Bulgaria combined, or the size of the seven New England states from Maine to New Jersey. At this rate, by the year 2000 there will be only two small patches left in Africa and South America.

Deserts are spreading at the rate of 24,000 square miles a year, a size one-third larger than Switzerland.

Fourth, humankind has to recognize that the burden of protecting the Common Heritage is a common one. A hen and a pig look at a human's breakfast of eggs and bacon in different ways: for one it is a passing event but for the other it is a total commitment—a sacrifice of livelihood. In the protection of forests, likewise, some people whose livelihood depends on logging will invariably be threatened. It is necessary, then, for townspeople to go beyond opposing logging. Adequate compensation has to be paid to people who will lose out financially by a ban on logging.

Finally, all of the work will need to be coordinated at the global level. There is, then, a need for an international agency to do the global priority-setting and to handle the compensation payments. Almost all international agencies consist only of governments. I suggest that the proposed Common Heritage Commission contain not only all the world's governments but

---

Making rules to stop environmental destruction is one thing, but the Brundtland Report explores three additional considerations: 1) the development of alternative income sources for the people who are required to stop doing what they're doing, 2) education so people will understand and eventually demand protection of their environments, and 3) inspection and enforcement of the rules.

In response to the growing ills, we can expect (or at least hope) the early 21st century to bring some drastic changes to the basic structure of world society and the global ecosystem. Gas-burning cars will be phased out, paper use will be largely replaced by images on computer display screens, forests that are quickly disappearing today will be replanted and nurtured, world population will be stabilized, and integrating networks of fiberoptic communications and high-speed transportation and distribution will bring economic fairness and intellectual equity worldwide. The United Nations will evolve into a fairly strong and healthy world body that fairly represents the world's governments, industries and citizens' groups, and enforces its decisions with global support.

Meanwhile the biggest step we in the overdeveloped world need to take in the waning years of this century is to achieve greater efficiency in our insatiable use of resources by transforming societies to a sustainable pattern of development. Growth at any cost must become a thing of the past. At the same time we need to determine the most vital and basic portions of the planet that need protection from today's efficient methods of using the land.

—*MHM*

also representatives of two sectors whose work impacts on the earth: non-governmental movements (such as the environmental and peace ones) and transnational corporations.

No one leaves this planet alive. And it is the only one we have. The enlarged Common Heritage concept will guarantee that the planet remains in good hands to see us into the planet's new era.

Chapter Thirteen:
Beyond the Brundtland Report

by Hilkka Pietila

Her background. Former secretary-general Finnish UN Association (1963-90). Member and official in many national and international groups, including Women for Mutual Security, Women for Peace, and International Foundation of Development Alternatives (IFDA). Extensive international involvement in seminars, conferences and study groups on all continents. Several hundred articles and major presentations on development, peace, human rights and women's issues. Fluency in Finnish, Swedish and English, passable German.

Her chapter. If the concept of sustainable development, which is the core notion of the Brundtland Report, is to be taken seriously, the whole philosophy of economics and the characteristics of cultivation economy need to be studied. The role of unpaid labor, primarily that of women, as well as nonmonetized subsistence and household economies should be recognized as an integral part of human economy.

When we speak about basic needs and nutrition we already have a women's perspective on development.

Beyond the Brundtland Report

by Hilkka Pietila

The Brundtland Report successfully made environmental issues a world concern. It came none too soon and, hopefully, in time. Awareness of the rapid deterioration of the environment was, however, already strongly expressed in the documents adopted at the United Nations Conference on Human Environment in 1972, and in the World Conservation Strategy prepared by United Nations Environment Programme (UNEP), International Union for Conservation of Nature and Natural Resources (IUCN) and World Wildlife Fund (WWF) in 1980.

It is regrettable that the message was not taken seriously in the early 1970s because then it would have been so much easier to handle the issues, and at least some of the perhaps irreparable damage which has taken place since then would have been avoided. But is the Brundtland Report more acceptable than its predecessors because of its moderation, or has the situation finally become so bad that hardly anyone can deny the seriousness of the problems?

A lot of lip service is paid to the Brundtland Report without a proper reading to see what is in the report and what it lacks. Officially, Nordic countries have accepted and taken the report most favourably. There is, however, a lot of criticism of the report in these countries as well, not because of what the report says, but primarily because 1) it is too cautious, 2) it is internally contradictory, and 3) it ignores the role of women in the management of environmental issues and in their potential to be agents of change in a new direction.[1]

Limits to Growth

It is quite generally agreed that the Brundtland Report does assess the situation accurately but the recommendations of what should be done, and how, are not consistent with the drastic diagnosis. This weakness may be due to the political, don't-make-waves backgrounds of the commissioners or to a lack of analysis and insight, or to both.

The approach of the Brundtland Commission is the prevailing one: Nature is seen only as the property of humankind, as resources and raw materials for economic activity. The relationship of man and nature is not discussed and thus the consideration of ethical and aesthetic aspects of this relationship are also missing. The underlying notion seems to be man as Lord of Nature, rather than as a part of living nature.

Recognition of the value of living nature and of nature as an environment of culture and human existence is totally missing. Also missing is all history of development, and analyses: how and why we arrived where we are now. The symptoms are recognized, but the causes are not sought or studied. The roots of maldevelopment remain untouched. This is perhaps one of the reasons that the recommendations are so poor.

The harshest criticism the report has received has been because of its stand concerning economic growth. It proposes continuous economic growth everywhere, in rich as well as poor countries, and has even made it a prerequisite of sustainable development. This notion is not consistent with existing knowledge about and experience of international development. The growth of the rich has not benefited the poor.

The Brundtland Commission makes a similar mistake as the report to the Club of Rome, *Limits to Growth*, made in the 1970s.[2] The report did not distinguish where economic growth should be halted and where it is still necessary for a long time. The Brundtland Report makes the same mistake but in reverse; it does not separate industrialized countries from Third World countries, but proposes that economic growth continue everywhere. Thus it negates its own goal of more just international development.

Economic growth—the growth of production and consumption of goods—in rich countries today and in the future only implies increasing waste of natural resources and destruction of the environment, and by no means sustainable development. Enrichment of contemporarily rich countries and sustainable development are mutually exclusive goals. The damage done by an unabated and indiscriminate economic growth cannot be restored by additional growth.

Seemingly, for obvious reasons—the relationships of the commissioners with their political and other background structures—there is very little discussion about power systems, which maintain and aggravate unsustainable growth everywhere. The Commission makes suggestions to governments and inter-governmental agencies, but ducks the key issues, like the power of transnational corporations, which operate without impediment through international trade. Transnational corporations efficiently utilize international disparities and do not care about the environment of any country. They barely follow the legal provisions for the protection of nature in countries where there are such provisions, and skillfully transport hazardous production and waste into countries where environmental legislation is poor or not well monitored.

In the field of security and environment, the Commission expresses itself quite boldly and unambiguously. It recognizes the connection between nuclear power and the proliferation of nuclear weapons and it does not trust the International Atomic Energy Agency (IAEA) as an organization to control the development of nuclear technology for so-called "peaceful uses." "We recommend in the strongest terms the construction of an effective international regime covering all dimensions of the (nuclear) problem. . . . This should be quite separate from the role of IAEA in promoting nuclear energy." This is a clear vote of no-confidence for the IAEA and a serious warning against visualizing nuclear power as a solution to energy problems.

What Is Sustainable Development?

The core notion of the Brundtland Report is sustainable development, which is defined by the Commission as "development that meets the needs of the present without compromising the ability of future generations to meet their own needs." According to the Commission, it contains two key concepts:

• the concept of "needs," in particular the essential needs of the world's poor, to which overriding priority should be given;

• the idea of limitations imposed by the state of technology and social organization on the environment's ability to meet present and future needs.

With the first point, the Commission assumes a rightful goal of more just global development. But the second point seems to be reversed. Is it not rather the environment, the terms of living nature, which set the limits, and not the state of technology and social organization? To a laywoman, this point seems to indicate that the Commission has stumbled over its words in its very basic definition. How can this have happened?

This definition of the main concepts does express a goal of sustainable development, but it says nothing about the conditions and modes of operation by which this type of development would become a reality. The basic theory or philosophy of sustainable development is missing in the report and thus the entire concept is left hanging in midair.

The issue is naturally the relationship of humanity with nature -the relationship of human economy today, particularly industrial economy with the economy of nature, i.e. ecology. Here the notion of sustainable development bumps heads with economics as a science, which does not count nature until it is converted into money: raw materials, work of extraction or cultivation and even damage is counted in national economics only as it entails the use of money. Still, development thinking is primarily—almost exclusively—based on this inadequate economics. Therefore, the whole of economics needs to be rethought for the purposes of sustainable development.

Inadequate Economics

One major shortcoming of prevailing economics is its inability to distinguish the cultivation economy from the extraction or industrial economy (see Figures 2 and 3).

Cultivation economy means all work and production which operates on living things like plants, trees and animals—that is, living resources. This economy produces basic commodities in cooperation with living nature. Agriculture, forestry, animal husbandry, fishing and all indigenous livelihoods belong to this type of economy. It can also be called a living economy.

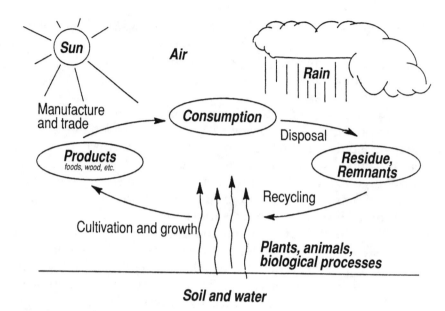

***Figure 2: Cultivation Economy
(a living economy)***

Renewable
Limited control, unpredictable
Monetization partial, important inputs free (sun, air and water)
Sustainable
Rhythm of life and nature
Mechanization limited
Longevity good
Competitiveness poor
Limited increase of efficiency and productivity

Extraction economy is primarily based on nonrenewable natural resources, minerals and fossils, which are dead materials extracted from the earth. This is the basis of industrial economy, though the raw materials produced by cultivation economy are also manufactured by industry. This economy is hardly dependent on the terms of living nature, thus its productivity and efficiency can be developed almost endlessly. Its driving force is profitability. (It can also be called a dead economy or simply a money economy.)[3]

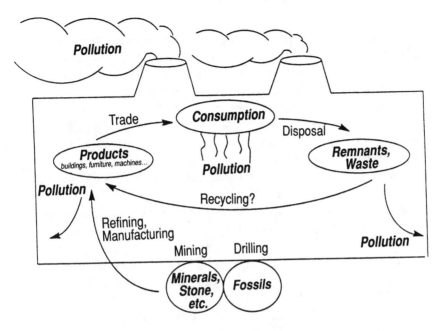

Figure 3: Extraction Economy (a dead or money economy)

Nonrenewable
Controllable and predictable
Fully monetized
No long-range sustainability
Rhythm of technology
Fully mechanized
Longevity poor
Competitiveness good
Ongoing increase of efficiency and productivity

When the terms of extraction economy are applied to the cultivation economy and the same demands of efficiency and productivity set on agriculture and husbandry as on industry, the system is bound to run into difficulties. National and international economies have been run in this way for as long as any intentional economic policies have been exercised. This is the main reason that the world economy is in the situation it is in today.

The existing cultivation economies—both the major proportion of Third World countries as primarily agricultural producers, and the agriculture of industrialized countries—are in insurmountable trouble. Third World countries have fallen into enormous debt and regression. Agriculture in industrialized countries, in spite of the application of the most advanced technology and significant subsidies, is about to collapse from debt and the effects of insane cultivation practices. This may also be one of the basic reasons for the rapid emigration of people from the rural areas and thus for the unmanageable growth of urban problems. Ultimately, all these consequences fall upon the environment and destroy the foundation of cultivation economy and human economy as a whole.

Another basic shortcoming of the prevailing economies is their total omission of unpaid labor and production in the household and subsistence economies. These economies are, in fact, the direct production of the welfare of people. All other welfare, provided with private or public funds, is indirect.[4]

This non-monetary part of a household, or family economy, is also extremely relevant from the sustainable development point of view. Originally, this economy was very prudent in its use of resources—due to plain necessity—and in many countries much of the traditional know-how of life and economy, with due respect to nature, has been preserved. Indeed, the environmental movements, particularly in many Third World countries, are extensively based on this knowledge.

We have good reason to question whether economies become more destructive as they become more monetized. Monetization also means a transference of power from people to impersonal collective structures. Industrialization and monetization of life have always, no matter where, implied the disempowerment of women.

Another important point is made by Ali Mazrui in his recent paper (1988).[5] "On the whole, capitalism has become more masculine as it became more internationalized; it also became more masculine as it became more mechanized." One can add that both of these processes have also made industrialized economies more and more insensitive to ecological aspects.

All this is also built into the background of the basic commodity negotiations and Uruguay-Round of General Agreement on Tariffs and Trades (GATT) negotiations. The conciliation between the basic commodity producers, the cultivation economies, and industrialized extraction economies is, because of their different natures, almost impossible.

When Third World countries, with their basic commodities, try to compete in world trade with manufactured products of extraction economies, the end results are further impoverishment of the poor, aggravation of food problems, and the deterioration of the environment, all becoming totally unmanageable. And still, the conditions of International Monetary Fund (IMF) and the World Bank virtually force Third World countries in this direction.

Food or Commodities?

International trade is the main battlefield of economic relations between South and North. There have been two aspects absent during all negotiations in United Nations Conference on Trade and Development (UNCTAD) and GATT, as well as concerning all commodity issues.

One disregarded aspect is the special nature of all cultivation production; in trade, agricultural products are considered equal to minerals and fossils. The second totally disregarded fact is the nutritional importance of the commodity; food products are lumped in the same category as pulp and paper, tobacco and coffee. Hence, people's basic needs have been risked to increase export income.

This kind of undiversified thinking in trade is certainly one consequence of the prevailing economic thought, where the leading principle is solely the monetary value of exchange. All business interactions are taking place as if the participating partners—companies, government delegations, international experts, etc.—were blind to the superior importance of products necessary for human life and the preservation of nature. The inability to solve the food problems in Third World countries is, to quite an extent, a consequence of this very blindness of the prevailing economic and business mechanisms.

Particularly shocking are the views, strongly emphasized in the fora of international trade negotiations, that industrialized countries should stop all support to their agriculture and lift the import barriers to allow Third World countries' agricultural products easier access to the markets of rich countries. This is fine perhaps for everything else, but not for products of basic need.

Concerning food, it would mean that rich industrialized countries would give up their own food production and instead import food from the South, where cheap and hungry labor will produce food for rich and fat Northerners. It would perhaps make food cheaper for us in the North—in spite of additional transportation and processing costs—but too expensive for the people who grow it. This will not promote sustainable development anywhere; neither will it bring about more just distribution of wealth!

Two questions arise: Would this be sensible use of land in the South? Would it be sensible to make industrialized countries totally dependent on the food production of the Third World? This could lead to a shifting of hunger problems, in the not so distant future, to the North, or to such an increase in food prices on the world market that those Third World countries importing food would starve even worse than now.

In a recent study by the International Institute for Applied Systems Analysis (IIASA), *Towards Free Trade in Agriculture*, the conclusion is "that most Organisation for Economic Co-operation and Development (OECD) countries would gain significant economic benefits over the next decade from a GATT Uruguay-Round agreement to reduce their agricultural tariffs, and quotas, but many developing countries would suffer as a consequence." Higher world market prices can benefit Third World countries exporting agricultural products, but they will contribute to hunger to those importing agricultural products.

"Net benefits . . . are the sum of positive effects on farmers producing for the market (the larger ones, usually) and negative effects on consumers (many of whom are poor and at the margin of minimum food needs)."

To speak in general about the agricultural products of the South is very confusing. One should diversify into at least the following categories of agricultural products:

• raw materials for industry (cotton, rubber, jute, timber, etc.);

• luxuries, primarily for Northern markets (coffee, tea, tobacco, cocoa, sugar, etc.);

• food and feed products (grain, rice, fruits, meat, groundnuts, soya, etc.).

Particular attention should be focused on the second category which takes huge areas of the best arable land but are no one's basic need.

From a basic human point of view, these categories vary in importance. If food production were a universal priority, as it should be, food problems would have been solved a long time ago. However, since priorities are defined according to the commercial value of products, the world's food problems persist.

Meaningful priorities and prices do not usually coincide! Products of basic need should be cheap and easily available to everyone and luxury products should be so expensive that only a small proportion of the land used for them today would be able to produce the same income. Food should not in principle be an ordinary commodity at all, but a utility secured for everyone.

This is approximately what a nutritional perspective of trade would imply. From the basic needs point of view, every country should be as self-reliant as possible in the satisfaction of basic needs. Self-reliant food production in industrialized countries would mean that imported input should be decreased to a minimum, as should chemical fertilizers and industrially produced feed for animals. If and when cultivation and production become ecologically as sound as possible, surpluses will vanish and thus so will the need to export to the world market. World trade would then consist primarily of products of secondary importance, which will not make countries fatally dependent upon each other.

The Brundtland Commission still believes in the benefits of free trade and the comparative advantage of markets without distinction of the varying importance of different products. The concept of the New International Economic Order is not mentioned at all.

Women's Perspective

When we speak about basic needs and nutrition we already have a women's perspective on development. Particularly in Africa, women are in a key position to provide food for people and to take responsibility for a major part of agricultural work in general. They also have a very prominent role in the so-called informal economy, which seems to be a lifeline when formal economy faces major difficulties. If women had the power to set priorities in production and trade, the basic needs of people and the self-reliance of the country would get the emphasis they deserve.

The export-oriented development in many countries has, however, been very detrimental to women in recent years. Women's access to land has diminished and thus it has become more and more difficult for them to provide food for their families. They often have to do most of the work, even on the cash-crop producing fields, without appropriate tools and training. Development for them has meant more work, less food, and no money, as usual!

Women in the South have the closest link with the environment, with water, land and forests. They are the ones who directly suffer because of the deterioration of the environment. Lack of clean water and the increasing distances from which water must be carried and firewood collected are the everyday reality of rural women in many countries. Still their pivotal position in relation to nature has not been recognized in the World Commission on Environment and Development (WCED) report, nor in the Environmental Perspectives to the Year 2000 and Beyond.

When one does recognize the role of women in environmental issues, it may be misinterpreted, as has been the case with firewood. The use of firewood by families is sometimes considered a major reason for deforestation. According to e.g. the first update of the UN World Survey on the Role of Women in Development, this assumption is false. "The collection of fuelwood in rural areas is not a major cause of deforestation. The main causes are large scale lumbering, agricultural expansion, overuse of existing agricultural land, burning of forests to encourage fodder growth, and over-grazing. Rapid urban growth also puts pressure on land." This new World Survey sheds a lot of light on issues concerning women and the environment.

Thanks to women's research, there is a great deal of evidence today about the commonality of the fate of women and nature. Techno-industrial development, with capital accumulation as a paramount aim, has been and continues to be constantly disastrous for both. Women and nature have been seen as resources to be utilized and exploited, even raped. Therefore, women's approach to nature and life is also very different than that of "the Lords of Nature". It is based on women's experiences of life as well as experiences of the process of so-called development. It therefore stems from a very different world view and system of values. Well-known examples of this approach are the work of women of the Chipko movement in India, the Greenbelt movement in Kenya and many others.[6]

The international women's movement is the biggest alternative movement in the world today. The subtle, often unconscious women's culture could be a rich, untapped and fresh source of values, practices and skills for alternative development, where people and nature would be treated with the respect and care they are due.[7] Therefore, it is a great pity that such an authoritative report, as the Brundtland Report, omits the potentiality of women's culture to provide practical and philosophical recipes for sustainable development.

An Ailing World Needs a Mother's Care

There were two young sisters bickering over the last orange. Dad, annoyed by the disruption and determined to solve the problem expediently, cut the orange in halves and gave one to each sister. The girls were still uncomfortable with the situation, which had not been fully resolved. Then Mom came by. Delving into the problem, she learned that one sister wanted to make marmalade from the peel; the other sister wanted to eat the meat of the orange. So Mom divided the fruit appropriately, giving the entire peel to one, all the flesh to the other, making both girls happy.

The world requires sensible, fair development plans, worked out case by case between interacting nations, whether they are involved in a dispute or in trade. Mechanical reactions to world crises and rigid political policies are inadequate. Financial assistance cannot solve problems unless it is accompanied by a well thought-out plan adequately addressing the needs of all parties. Devising such plans requires substantially more care, time and effort than the more expedient solutions in fashion today, such as applying money to a problem and assuming it will solve itself.

This fair approach which delves into the diversified needs of involved parties is often regarded as the feminine approach. Mechanical, rule-oriented solutions are considered masculine in nature. While both approaches have their value, it is certainly time for more feminine influence in world affairs.

—MHM

A Suggestion

In international debate there sometimes appears the notion that the concerns about the environment in the process of development are new tricks of industrialized countries to hamper the progress of the South. There are also real indications that rich countries or rather companies from these countries—have exported and continue their attempts to export some of their environmental problems to the Third World.

But in fact, we all know today's environmental problems are universal. The issues are both drought, desertification and erosion in the Third World and the creeping death of the forests, increasing pollution of the air, and acidity of lakes and rivers in the North. The greenhouse-effect and damage to the ozone layer threaten us all, not to mention the pile-up of holocaust weapons.

"The time has come to break out of past patterns. Attempts to maintain social and ecological stability through old approaches will increase instability," says the Brundtland Commission.

Personally, I am convinced that, if the concept of sustainable development is going to be taken seriously, the whole philosophy of economics needs to be reconsidered. I suggest that at least the following steps should be taken in the fields of research and policy:

1. Further work on identification of the distinct characteristics and conditions of three main components/sectors of human economy:

• the unpaid labor in the households and subsistence economies for direct production of human welfare;

• the cultivation of renewable natural resources, i.e. the production based on living potential of nature;

• the extraction and processing of nonrenewable natural resources, and processing the products of cultivation economy.

2. Research and analysis of the interplay and dynamics between these three areas of the totality of human economy.

3. Development of new methods and measures for taking these components of human economy into consideration in economic planning and policy making with due respect to their distinct characteristics and needs, and with the view of achieving sustainable development.

References and notes

1. Norwegian Research Council for Science and the Humanities, Nytt om Kvinneforskning (Oslo: Journal on Women's Research, Nr 2/88). Special issue on Brundtland Commission's Report: Elin Svenneby, "Med menneskene som udefinert malestokk" (Man as an undefined yardstick); Else Skjonsberg: "Var felles framtid?" (Our common future?); Sigrun Kaul, "Barekraftig utvikling—pa hvem sine skulde?" (Sustainable development—on whose shoulders?); Ebba Wergeland, "Med p-piller till de syltende" (P-pills for the starving).

2. D. Meadows & al, *Limits to Growth, Report to the Club of Rome* (New York: Universe Books, 1972) 205 pp.

3. Nicholas Georgescu-Roegen, Economic Theory and Agrarian Economics (Oxford Economic Papers, N.S.XII, Nr 1 February 1960) and "Process in Farming versus Process in Manufacturing: A Problem on Balanced Development," in Economic Problems of Agriculture in Industrial Societies (London: Ugo Papi & Charles Nunn, 1969).

4. Hilkka Pietila and Kyosti Puliainen, "Revival of Non-monetary Economy Makes Economic Growth Unnecessary (in Industrialized Countries)," IFDA Dossier 35, and "Tomorrow Begins Today. Elements for a Feminine Alternative in the North," IFDA Dossier 57/58. Also Marilyn Waring, *If Women Counted. A New Feminist Economics* (San Francisco: Harper & Row, 1988).

5. Ali Mazrui, The Uneven Development of Sovereignties: A Third World Perspective, unpublished paper presented at a World Order Models Project (WOMP) Seminar, in Moscow, USSR, 10-16 October 1988.

6. Jayanta Bandyopadhyay and Vandana Shiva, "Political economy of ecology movements," IFDA Dossier 71.

7. Hilkka Pietila, "Daughers of Mother Earth. Women's Culture as an ethical and practical basis for sustainable development," in J. Engel (ed), Ethics of Environment and Development (London: Belhaven Press, 1990).

More of Ms. Pietila's ideas can be found in her books, including:

Making Women Matter—the Role of the United Nations (Zed, London 1990)

Shift of Power—Women's Reflections on Politics, Economics and Future (Helsinki 1988)

In Defense of Human Dignity (Juva, 1981)

Anthologies:

"Daughters of Earth—Women's culture as a basis for sustainable development," in *Ethics of Environment and Development*, J. Engel (Belhaven, London 1990)

"Ecophilosophy and Feminism—A recipe for sustainable development," in *Biopolitics—the bio-environment*, A. Vlavianos (Athens 1988)

"International Cooperation," in *Teaching for International Understanding, Peace and Human Rights*, N. Graves (UNESCO 1984)

The Final Chapter:
Toward a Global Consensus

by Mark Macy

To help pull together the diverse ideas of this book, several main ideas were extracted from each chapter, compiled into a questionnaire and mailed off to the authors in hopes of drawing a consensus. Despite three obstacles—the complexity of some of the ideas, the limitations of the written word, and the fact that everyone views life and the world a bit differently—the survey produced many important and interesting results.

To broaden the consensus, I invited the authors of my previous anthology, *Solutions for a Troubled World*, to participate in the survey for this book. Following are the *Solutions* authors who helped out:

- Ahmad Abubakar, economic planner, Nigeria
- Archie Bahm, retired professor, peace activist and author of *The World's Living Religions* (Dell), USA
- John Fobes, president of Americans for the Universality of UNESCO, USA
- Chellis Glendinning, psychologist and author of *Waking Up in the Nuclear Age* (William Morrow 1987), USA
- Louis Kriesberg, sociology professor and author, USA
- Howard Richards, professor, attorney and author, USA
- Jan Tinbergen, economist and Nobel laureate, the Netherlands
- Jan van der Linden, president of the School for Esoteric Studies, USA and the Netherlands
- Caesar Voute, lecturer, adviser and retired professor, the Netherlands
- Rene Wadlow, world federalist and editor of *Transnational Perspectives*, Switzerland and USA

The authors rated each issue on a seven-point scale:
I strongly agree (3 points)
I think so (2 points)
It makes sense (1 points)
No opinion (0 points)
I'm skeptical (-1 points)
I think not (-2 points)
I strongly disagree (-3 points)

Herein are the results of the issues that were rated above 50 percent. Why 50 percent? Simply because that indicates fairly strong agreement. To illustrate:

• 100 percent consensus would require all authors to have voted 3. The highest actual score turned out to be 93 percent on the statement that children need love, emotional connection and encouragement to wonder.

• Total disagreement (all voting -3), would have yielded a score of -100%. Only one issue in the survey dipped into the negative (-16%), this being a proposal to require a parenting license before having children. Dr. Bernie Siegel recommends this in the Prologue with tongue just partly in cheek as a possible means of eliminating the widespread problems of abused and neglected children. Despite its logical merits, the notion that parents should have to demonstrate effective parenting skills to some licensed authority to ensure balanced kids and stable families strikes a sour note in societies where family-building is left largely to personal discretion. As the problems brought on by increased growth and consolidation multiply around the globe in the coming decades, perhaps the notion of parenting licenses will gain greater favor. Perhaps they will become the western world's answer to intensive, society-wide family planning programs that have helped countries in the Far East to achieve greater social balance and economic momentum since the 1950s.

• If all authors had voted 1 to indicate moderate agreement, the score would be only 33 percent, and the issue would be excluded from this chapter. Such lukewarm agreement was reached on a few items that concerned ideas unfamiliar to most authors, such as 1) the benefits of balanced Qi (life force) in personal healing, 2) the drawbacks of being alienated from one's divine essence or god potential (which seems to be a major problem in industrialized societies), 3) the notion that spontaneous remission of cancer can occur when a patient's life is suddenly rebuilt upon unconditional love, and 4) the idea that many ills of society and planet can be alleviated through meditation.

In any case, the issues listed herein are those which received hearty agreement.

Authors were invited to write in additional comments beside issues that stirred their interest. The most controversial issue, the one that drew the most comments, was a statement by Robert Muller: "We are on the threshold of a wonderful era; a truly great period of human fulfillment, interdependence, love and community is now about to begin."

> *Hazel Henderson responded: "We could be!"*
>
> *Howard Richards: "I want to think so."*
>
> *Joseph Schaeffer: "We hope so!"*
>
> *Jan van der Linden: "But we have to work for it."*
>
> *John Fobes: "It may require several generations and much pulling and hauling."*
>
> *Caesar Voute: "It needs a common effort in very complicated processes. If only we can respond to a unique challenge."*
>
> *Archie Bahm, less optimistic: "A catastrophic era, perhaps?"*
>
> *Chellis Glendinning points out that "plutonium has a half-life of 250,000 years!!"*

This issue drew a meager 17 percent consensus. I include it here not only because of its controversial nature, but also because I tend to believe that we are indeed entering a wonderful age of humanity, and I suspect it may involve as rapid and dizzying a process as the reconsolidation of Eastern Europe.

HEALING OUR LIVES

1. Many obstacles hinder our efforts to heal our lives.

Among the biggest obstacles to physical healing is a weak immune system. This can be caused by a wide range of conditions, including poor nutrition, genetic defects, lack of self-esteem, stress, lack of love, emotional imbalances, lack of exercise, and unhappiness. (73)

Robert Muller would add pessimism, frustration and hopelessness.
Chellis Glendinning would add such external influences as the
deteriorating ozone layer, toxic exposure, and radiation.
Hazel Henderson would add poverty.
Ahmad Abubakar: "In my opinion, stress arising from impatience
and greed of modern living and processed foods with too much
chemical content are the major causes. Restlessness is another
important cause—too much prolonged activity."
Howard Richards points out: "The immune system cannot be
expected to work well in a highly artificial environment. We need
to design natural environments composed of substances which
evolution has fitted the human body to deal with. However, it is
also true that research can detect the mechanisms of the immune
system and lend to measures that are healthy even though not
traditional and not natural."
Philosopher Archie Bahm would turn the table: "A person may
acquire too much immunity. At my age (83), too many antibodies
in my lungs aggravate my asthma; (they may kill me!)"

While western civilization is becoming skilled at measuring
the energies within us (using, for example, EEGs, thermal
photography, and bacterial growth analysis) Westerners lack (or,
perhaps, have lost) much of the skill to use or feel their inner
power. (51)

Nor do we use and feel the full vitality of the human being, adds
Robert Muller.
Rene Wadlow: "I think one should not overestimate the loss of such
skills in the West. They exist in many individuals but are seldom
discussed."
Howard Richards: "The price of commercial success has been distance
between the body and the spirit."

Growing up in a family which does not meet our emotional
needs, especially our need for generous portions of unconditional
love, can lead to adulthood emotional imbalances. (82)

John Fobes prefers the term unselfed love and stresses the need to
interpret family broadly.
Howard Richards: "Healthy families make healthy communities,
and vice versa."

Chellis Glendinning: "The dysfunctional family (being such an important subject today), addictive-codependent process analysis and treatment has arisen as one of the most helpful and insightful."

The unbridled ego, or "I" feeling, can be an obstacle to spiritual pursuit and enlightenment. (86)

Rene Wadlow: "Of course, it depends on what one means by the ego."

John Fobes: "I agree, but let's get the ego out of the self. That concept is fragmenting and springs from a perverse human desire to limit and control life."

Archie Bahm warns: "The word spiritual . . . has many meanings. (If it means) wholesomeness, why not use the term wholesome? If it means immanence of theos, then many issues remain to be resolved. (There is a) history of vicious religious wars, and these continue today, wrecking Beirut, Lebanon, etc., etc. Although every religion claims to aim at peace, each also wants peace on its own terms—often enough to insist on fighting for them."

Howard Richards recalls a quote from Rabindranath Tagore: "Make of my life an empty reed that thou might fill me with music."

Hilkka Pietila is unsure of the meaning of unbridled ego. She wonders, "Is it that inflated male ego which is so common? The female ego is most often obstructed!"

Most individuals in modern society have been alienated from their divine essence. (51)

Howard Richards: "Modern economic society by definition treats humans and their labor power as commodities, not as sacred entities."

John Fobes feels the statement may be true for more than just "modern society."

Rene Wadlow agrees with Mr. Fobes: "(It's) true of all societies." And he adds, "This is why the soul is reincarnated. If he were already one with the whole, he would not be here."

This spiritual alienation is the *root* of a problem, but it is its symptoms—including neurological, emotional and many physical disorders—which get the bulk of our attention. (51)

Rene Wadlow: "Spiritual alienation is the nature of being human."

Howard Richards: "I would say rather it is one way of looking at the root of the problem. Spiritual alienation is both cause and consequence of commercialism. Either can be considered the root."

John Fobes concludes: "So our attention should be turned to our spiritual roots in order to counteract the alienation."

Many people acquire more and more material goods in a futile effort to gratify more basic needs for love and community that are not being met. (66)

John Fobes speculates: "or perhaps to avoid thinking about those basic needs."

On the other hand, Howard Richards replies: "There are more people who do not have their basic material needs met (because of) a failure of love and community."

Harmful customs and habits present a major obstacle to healing because it is usually difficult to break a familiar pattern. (80)

Howard Richards: "True, but humans are on the whole creatures of custom and habit. We cannot create a culture with an unconventional majority. We can only change the customs."

Hilkka Pietila points out that it is not always difficult to break habits.

But Chellis Glendinning observes: "Patterns are often so deeply rooted in psychic survival beliefs (in the unconscious), it takes a special process to break through."

Examples of harmful customs and habits:
• Poor dietary customs abound, including high fat consumption in overdeveloped societies, low protein intake in much of the Third World, and recreational use of alcohol, alkaloids (caffeine, nicotine, cocaine . . .) and other mild poisons. (76)
• Idleness is an easy trap for modern societies where physical exertion is not required in many people's day-to-day lives. (71)

Howard Richards: "St. Thomas Aquinas said apathy is a sin because it shows lack of love motivating people to serve God and other people."

Hilkka Pietila: "Idleness is not necessarily laziness."

• Following the news in modern societies where newspapers, TV and other media have a tradition of dwelling on crime and misfortune feeds us a daily barrage of unhealthy energy patterns. (65)
• Watching programs and movies and listening to songs filled with messages of violence and promiscuity tell our body-mind that we live in an unhealthy world, and we start to think and behave accordingly. (60)

> *Howard Richards: "(US) media are in principle irresponsible because they do what attracts attention in order to get high ratings and advertising dollars."*

• Thinking negatively about oneself or one's world tells the body-mind that life is not worth living. (69)

• Competitive societies are stressful. For an individual to accept chronic stress and its associated despair as normal gives the body a "die" message, causing our immune system to weaken and to allow us to become ill. (56)

> *Howard Richards: "The problem is to make a cooperative society work. On the other hand, a certain degree of competition can be fun, as in intermural volleyball or sandlot softball."*

2. Each of us is ultimately in charge of healing our own life.

> *Caesar Voute: "Unfortunately, one is often exposed to external influences which one cannot control!"*
> *Howard Richards: "Alcoholics Anonymous has the right idea: we need a Higher Power."*
> *Ahmad Abubakar: "Family and society/community can help a lot."*

Complete healing includes:
• eating well (77)
• minimizing or eliminating from our lives harmful recreational substances such as alcohol and alkaloids (caffeine, nicotine, cocaine, heroine. . .) (83)
• exercising (75)
> *Howard Richards: "It doesn't have to be strenuous."*
> *Hilkka Pietila: "Moderately."*
• hearing and seeing mostly positive stimuli in news, movies, magazines, books, etc. (78)
> *John Fobes adds, "and in other people."*
> *Howard Richards: "(For most people to achieve such positive awareness) would require cultural changes; we are each responsible for each other's dreams."*
• positive thinking (65)
> *Chellis Glendinning recommends "realistic thinking, whole thinking."*
> *Howard Richards: "Melancholia also has its functions, as Freud understood."*
• learning to minimize the effects of stress on our body-mind. (71)

The process can be made easier if we can:
- open our heart to unconditional love (71)

Howard Richards: "This can be done by actions."
- learn to get in touch with the Divine Essence or God Potential

in each of us (54)

" *... and in the community," Howard Richards adds.*

Majid Rhanema emphasizes that this idea (which comes from his chapter) does not necessarily reflect his own personal views. He clarifies: "I personally believe that we are all parts of a wider reality which transcends our so-called material world, a reality which represents indeed a higher and different form of intelligence or energy. The dilemma of the human being is that, on the one hand, it is nothing but a tiny expression of this energy, and, on the other hand, it remains utterly unable to ever grasp or understand it in all its dimensions. This is why I always hesitate to give that energy or intelligence a name, be it God or anything else. For I feel that could only serve to trap the seekers of truth (or what is). As a rule, I prefer not to talk about God. Not only because I feel I should not talk about things I do not know, but, more particularly, because I guess the God most people believe in is nothing but an invention of their own religion or culture."

Love is a binding force of human life, making cells and tissues within us and social groups around us more cohesive, and it is a force that can help unify the world in peace. (67)

Caesar Voute: "This is how it should be, however it may not always work in this manner in our very complex world."

Howard Richards: "The problem is partly to make love practical in an economic world."

Fostering love within us is a vital step toward healing. (68)

Howard Richards: "I would say rather love among us."

Each of us has God potential, and it is in the best interest of our world and ourself to discover it and use it righteously. (61)

Rene Wadlow: "Some, of course, do not use the word God for this energy."

Learning the nature of our own internal forms of power can bring us greater health and peace. (67)

Howard Richards: "I would say that our forms of power are in our relaxedness to other people and the environment."

John Fobes points out that we don't own these powers; "they are part of the cosmic commons."

Inner contemplation and meditative visualization of a healthy body can help heal our lives. (52)

If we could divide human nature into its basic aspects and prioritize them in terms of their importance in creating a complete person, they could be the following qualities:
1) spiritual,
2) moral,
3) mental and
4) physical.
Modern education avoids the moral and spiritual aspects of children. Many adults must develop these aspects of themselves later in life in order to heal their lives. (58)

Most authors seemed to agree with the closing paragraph but several questioned the heirarchy. Chellis Glendinning wonders why emotional is left out. Hilkka Pietila sees importance in all the qualities, saying they need to be equal and in harmony. Ahmad Abubakar would reprioritize them as spiritual, physical, mental and moral, and he writes: "In Nigeria moral and spiritual education of children is still fairly strong."

Individuals who hold self-discovery and self-knowledge as an on-going, lifelong task become self-reliant. (72)

3. Our state of health is determined not only by conditions within us but by the world around us as well. Conversely, our state of health helps shape the world around us. (76)

Individuals who hold self-discovery and self-knowledge as an on-going lifelong task develop a deeper sense of relatedness to others. (74)

To be healthy, individuals must be happy and comfortable in their social groups (family, friendships, workplace, community, country, and world). (67)
Hilkka Pietila: "Not necessarily; not all the time."

Healing one's life often requires healing one's family relationships first. (59)

Howard Richards: "I would not discourage people whose relationships are past healing and need just to be accepted, (healthy or not)."

The world is greater than the sum of its parts—nations, religions, cultures and ecosystems. Gaining an understanding and love for the planet should be near the top of everyone's list of priorities. (82)

Learning the skills of the citizen diplomat would help people get along with other people (which in turn would make their own lives healthier). (70)

For a society to get out of a pattern of obsessive growth would require attitude changes among its individual members. (81)

Howard Richards: "The new attitudes need to be rewarded, the (system) needs to be geared toward sustainability, and toward encouraging individuals who have constructive attitudes."

• These attitude changes would include changing society's focus from economic growth to personal growth (meaning here not the satisfaction of one's material cravings but the achievement of genuine emotional, physical and spiritual well-being). (69)

• It would mean fostering the Divine Essence within us, accepting the resulting powers and using them wisely. (63)

Archie Bahm warns of semantical problems: "(If divine means) Nature, Tao or Qi, why not use those terms. If it means something revealed by Hebraic, Christian or Islamic scriptures and theologies, then, since armies have been inspired by such divinity, it can be most dangerous ... "

Howard Richards concurs: "I wonder whether it will be possible to get worldwide consensus on this language. Practice will tell us which phrases are widely acceptable."

In this era of vanishing resources and environmental destruction, sustainable development (the satisfaction of everyone's basic needs and the growth and maintenance of society in a way that preserves environmental integrity) as a social policy and a personal way of life must become ingrained in everyone's mind. This would help each of us to feel at peace with Nature and, hence, more at peace with ourself. (92)

Robert Muller considers one of the most important steps toward planetary healing to be "simple and frugal living; live simply so that others may simply live."

HEALING OUR SOCIETIES

1.There are many obstacles in the way of healing our societies.

Many societies acquire more and more resources in a futile effort to gratify their members' basic needs for love and community, which are lacking. (59)

> *Howard Richards would rephrase it: "Societies have not found ways to create environments where spiritual satisfactions grow, and mistakenly view problems in material terms."*

• China is a population of intelligent, diligent, courageous individuals accustomed to hardships and lingering, outmoded traditions ruling much of their lives. These qualities exist today, presenting a substantial challenge for the future.

> *Archie Bahm points out that not all Chinese traditions are outmoded; "some are the best in the world."*

Women and Nature have been regarded as resources to be utilized and exploited. (69)

> *Chellis Glendinning: "(Mostly) by men in power and by male culture."*
>
> *Caesar Voute: "Unfortunately!"*
>
> *Howard Richards: "Not just regarded, also treated."*
>
> *Jan van der Linden adds that men (labor) have been exploited too, by Economic Man.*

Modern society has helped to alienate its members from their divine essence and, in doing so, has severed their sense of relatedness. This is the root of a problem whose many symptoms include crime, poverty, envy and greed. While the solution to the problem lies in the relationship between individuals and their divine essence, it is the symptoms that get the bulk of our attention. (57)

> *Caesar Voute adds: "An open-minded Westerner living in an Eastern society cannot but deplore the way we have developed over the centuries."*
>
> *Howard Richards: "The solution has other names (besides divine essence), such as Martin Luther King's beloved community. I think this statement is true; the problem is, putting it this way may take the focus away from global structures and from relaxedness."*

Joseph Schaeffer has a problem not only with the term but with the concept: "(It is) part of the problem, this idea of divine essence."

2. To heal our societies there are many facts to keep in mind.

The family is the most basic social system. Present in virtually all communities and societies throughout history, it has always been the most important institution for perpetuating values, building self-esteem, instilling a sense of commitment to others, and providing social stability. (78)

Chellis Glendinning is skeptical about just how basic family is: "I think the tribe or community may be more important in indigenous cultures."

Caesar Voute reminds us, "The family encompasses more than husband, wife, parents and children. The extended family concept needs to be protected."

John Fobes takes a broader spiritual tack: "It follows that the concept (of family) should be manifested at all levels of the universe, reflecting that all beings are children of one divine father/mother."

Family relationships and family security prepare us to deal with the larger world in acceptable ways. (88)

Majid Rhanema: "Depends on the nature of these relationships."

Hazel Henderson warns, "Families also (can be) violent structures of oppression."

In China, children are revered as the most precious gifts of Nature. Children need:
- love and emotional connection. (93)
- their creativity and individuality fanned and fostered. (83)
  Howard Richards: "I am not sure it is a felt need in all cultures."
- encouragement toward their strengths. (89)
- to be taught to wonder, not to have their interest deadened. (93)
- to learn less how to memorize and more how to ask questions and to find answers. Teachers need not cover a subject, but uncover part of it. (78)

Howard Richards: "This is not good advice for all teachers and all students. Sometimes trying to follow it leads to learning little or nothing."

- to learn to communicate: to listen, speak and write. (89)
  Howard Richards feels that more basic forms of communication drama, song and dance—should come first.

• nurturing along their slow development path. (78)
• respect for and a sense of belonging in their environment. (89)
• reality training—winning and losing, suffering and pleasure, control and submission, thought and feelings. (74)
> *Howard Richards: "It may be better for parents to be unconditionally supportive and for the outside world to teach losing."*
• order and discipline. (82)
> *Majid Rhanema: "Depends on the meanings given these two words. An order and discipline which are not understood nor inwardly accepted do not have a positive effect on the learner."*

To be healthy, a family requires generous amounts of love, caring, nurturing, commitment, deep values, trust and discipline. (89) All economies, including competitive ones, are built on a stable base of grassroots trust and cooperation, volunteer work and parenting. (70)
> *Howard Richards: "Overly competitive ones destabilize their own bases."*

Some behavioral disorders of individuals (such as drug addiction, overeating disorders and neurosis) are comparable to problems of societies (such as petroleum craving, overconsumption of resources, and vicious circles of degenerating, self-deceptive behavior on the part of entire societies, such as the notion that growth and more growth will cure the economy). What we know about personal disorders can help us understand social and international problems. (52)
> *Howard Richards: "This makes sense if we bear in mind that social decisions are mainly made through economic mechanisms, such as money."*
> *Caesar Voute warns: "A resemblance does not mean that the same process is at work. Be careful in making such comparisons."*

There are myths surrounding growth:
• That growth will yield contentment is a myth. (In truth, it just perpetuates greater desire, more growth and discontentment. Contentment really comes from a sense of community, stable friendships and love in the family.) (78)
• That growth will eliminate poverty is a myth. (Actually, it is the rift between rich and poor, not the actual level of poverty, that makes people feel dissatisfied and "poor.") (61)

• That growth will heighten generosity is a myth. (In reality, greed and personal striving remain as strong as ever as products proliferate.) (67)

• That growth will provide the resources and technology to clean up the environment is a myth. (This is the ultimate social neurosis in overdeveloped countries—a vicious circle of growth and ravaging with the blind hope that a miracle cure will be born of the uncontrolled activity to solve the problems it creates. Actually unbridled growth harms the environment. Period.) (72)

3. There are many innovative ways to overcome the obstacles to healing society.

Families could be helped and stabilized with well-conceived support from society. (75)

> *Caesar Voute: "The problem lies in selecting the type of well conceived support—Western European or North American contexts."*

• When a family breaks down, it is in society's best interest to provide support to the family and its members while they get back on their feet. (61)

> *Howard Richards: "However it is illusory to expect that without social change families will get back on their feet."*

• It is in society's best interest to help keep families together, to eliminate child abuse, to reach a consensus on values worth nurturing, and to help troubled children. (81)

• Many women choose to work *and* raise children. It is in society's best interest to support these women by adopting generous maternity leave, medical care and daycare policies. (65)

> *Howard Richards: "The problem is to find the resources to do it; the solution may be in voluntary service."*
>
> *Caesar Voute: "In our age this is the best way to integrate women fully in today's and tomorrow's society."*
>
> *Hilkka Pietila emphasizes that parenting is a shared role of fathers and mothers, and these policies should reflect that sharing.*

• It is in society's best interest to ensure that individuals and families have access to jobs and economic security, health care, child care, elder care, family leave, services for elderly, quality education, equal opportunity, equal compensation for equal work, shelter, and safe neighborhoods and cities. (77)

Caesar Voute: "It should be technically and economically feasible, otherwise we are trapped by our over-optimistic idealism."

Howard Richards: "This is all true but I doubt that paying civil servants more money to implement those goals is enough. A new spirit and revised structures are needed."

Robert Muller reminds us that the UN has proclaimed 1994 as the International Year of the Family, indicating that the spirit and new structures are growing.

• Society-wide mobilization of planned parenting organizations at various levels from neighborhood to nation can help instill needed family values throughout society. (52)

Howard Richards suggests that this "should be done building on existing organizations."

Caesar Voute adds: "(This is) the ideal case; reality in the West is still far from this."

Chellis Glendinning agrees: "There is the society-we'd-like-to-live-in, and there are the temporary strategies to get us there. I hope this is one of the latter."

Education in industrialized society largely ignores the spiritual and moral aspects of character development. Schools as well as families should help nurture all four aspects of our nature. (84)

Mass ecological education is vital. A generation aware of environmental problems will provide the needed momentum to correct them. (92)

Caesar Voute: "No time to lose!"

Howard Richards: "Not unless the education also shows how to make a saner society work. Ecological awareness only shows the problems—not the solutions."

Permanently healing a society will require education that teaches all children love and respect for self, society and planet. (86)

Robert Muller points out that this is especially true when it comes to healing world society.

Grassroots unrest is starting to shape government policy in many countries through activism. (61)

Caesar Voute: "A fact of life in the 1990s. If people at the grassroots lack relevant information and act on purely emotional grounds this can lead to a dangerous situation. We must emphasize the information processes!"

Ahmad Abubakar: "Governments are characterised by inertia and self-interest. It often takes damage of life and property and a lot of time to change their policies."

There are treatments available to alleviate unbridled growth:

• A change in our focus from economic growth to personal growth (meaning here not the satisfaction of one's material cravings but the achievement of genuine emotional, physical and spiritual well-being). (77)

Chellis Glendinning recommends changing focus to "social connectedness and nature connectedness" as well as personal growth.

• Cleaner, more energy-efficient and healthful transportation. (82)

Howard Richards: "The difficulty is to keep the economy going while shutting down certain parts of the auto and energy industries."

Hilkka Pietila favors restructuring society in a way that reduces the needs for transportation.

• Refining the arts, recreation and education. (78)

Caesar Voute: "Under education: how to use leisure time and serve society."

• Fostering a sense of community. (94)

Howard Richards: "To get a sense of community one must have a real community. Therefore we need to care for people's needs."

• Bringing psychological considerations to bear in our political systems. (57)

• In a neighborhood or village setting, changing emphasis from the pursuit of wealth to community-building brings greater enthusiasm and happiness and, ironically, more economic prosperity. (77)

Caesar Voute: "But how about the urban setting where the problems are much more serious?"

Howard Richards: "I would sacrifice economic prosperity if necessary—and I would measure it differently from the ways it is usually measured."

There are benefits that each style of medicine (Chinese and Western) could derive from the other. (75) Western science should investigate Chinese methods of healing and objectively determine their usefulness in the West. (72)

Ahmad Abubakar: "I would prefer the Chinese type since it is preventive, more natural, cheaper, and less destructive of resources and environment. It is less capital-intensive."

Luxury products (such as liquor, tobacco and coffee) should be more expensive to acquire. (75)

Women's culture should be examined as a rich, untapped, fresh source of values, practices and skills for alternative (sustainable) development. (67)

Rene Wadlow: "I have doubts about how different the attitudes of women are in practice, but a women's culture can be encouraged just in case."

Howard Richards feels that women's culture is not untapped, but rather is the basis of all culture, and he refers us to Nancy Tanner's book On Becoming Human.

Caesar Voute: "Women's culture should not be separated from men's culture. We should have one human culture (to avoid) segregation."

Robert Muller notes that feminine values need to play a larger role in government as well as in economics.

To update and replace economics we need to identify three basic components of human economy. We need to analyze their interactions (65):

1) unpaid labor (child-rearing, volunteer work)
2) cultivation of renewable resources
3) extraction of nonrenewable resources and processing of products. (70)

Self-knowledge strengthens one's extended cultural family and the sense of relatedness. Self-reliance comes to characterize communities composed of individuals who hold self-discovery and self-knowledge as a major lifelong task. (77)

The "achievements" of Swadhyaya communities in India are not fully measurable in the Western sense because their aim is not to achieve fragmented targets. However, Swadhyaya villages are superior to other villages in being clean, efficient, convivial and cooperative. There are lively expressions on people's faces and respectful, energetic relationships, especially between men and women.

*According to Majid Rhanema, self-knowledge in its broad, spiritual
sense is the only genuine way to heal self, society or world. Heal
may not even be a valid term. He writes: "Talking about healing
seems to me a contradiction in terms, as long as the healer is the
very source of the affliction or the malady he intends to heal. If we
live in a world of violence, fear, conflict, greed, alienation and
senseless reduction of life to economic needs, it is because we are
all that. No outer change of a political, technological or material
nature can alter that condition, per se. It is only the full
understanding of this fact that gives us the divine or transcendental
force enabling us to see ourselves as we are, rather than as we want
us to be. Healing is thus an exercise in awareness, a matter of
learning and listening to the world, of attending it, of looking at
what is, without any predefined image or conclusion, all of which
are essential to give us the necessary inner freedom to understand
reality and to act upon it."*

HEALING OUR PLANET

1. There is reason for optimism.

We have evolved from nomadic tribes, to settled communities
along rivers, to large agriculture-based societies. We are now
entering a fourth age in which we are seeing global limits to
territory and resources on the planet.

Interdependence and cooperation will be the guiding
principles of the new era. (61)

Changes are underway at the grassroots level toward greater
concern and kinship. (74)

Caesar Voute: "Indeed, awareness is increasing."

*Howard Richards: "I think so, but sometimes I think the reverse is
happening also."*

Love is a binding force of human life, making social groups
more cohesive and moving us toward a more unified, peaceful
world. (73)

Caesar Voute: "Love and solidarity . . . "

2. Before entering the new era, we have some serious problems to solve:

Competing nations have been ravaging the global commons, resulting in a damaged environment and unstable economy. (86)

In the process of becoming more internationalized and mechanized, capitalism has become more masculine and, hence, more insensitive to ecological concerns. (58)

An unsettling scenario has taken shape: The Industrialized world consumes Third World resources and gives back obsolete equipment, hazardous wastes and polluting industries. (67)

> *Rene Wadlow: "This is only a very partial picture of North-South relations."*
>
> *Howard Richards: "The Third World also pollutes. Burning wood for fuel is polluting. Environmental protection standards such as on auto emissions tend to be low in the Third World."*

Major crises today include drought, desertification, deforestation, overfishing, chemicalized agriculture, ravaged minerals, and poisoned air and waterways. (88)

Transnational corporations use the strengths and weaknesses of specific countries' policies (on such issues as toxic waste) to benefit themselves often at the expense of the environment. (65)

> *Rene Wadlow: "True, but this is not the only role of TNCs."*
>
> *Caesar Voute: "Capitalism isn't the only sinner; consider state enterprises in socialist countries."*

While market economics may have been a useful tool in rapidly building modern civilization, it is now dangerously outmoded and needs to be overhauled or replaced. (52)

> *Hazel Henderson stresses that it is not just market economics, but economic theories left and right that are outmoded.*
>
> *Caesar Voute: "Adaptation and adjustment to the new realities would be wiser; socialist economies have been even more damaging, as seen in Eastern Europe."*
>
> *Howard Richards feels that economics "can't be replaced; it needs to be recontextualized."*

Suffering is part of life. The heaviest burdens fall on shoulders at the bottom of society's pyramid. (57)

Rene Wadlow: "Suffering is probably in proportion to the tasks one faces. (Those on) the bottom often suffer from (nongratification) of physical needs; others in other ways."

Modern humanity has alienated itself from its divine essence and, in doing so, has severed the sense of relatedness among its member groups (nations, religions, transnational corporations, etc.). This is the root of a problem whose global symptoms include war, international inequities, unbridled growth and ravaged ecosystems. While solving the problem must include restoring ties between our selves and our divine essence, it is the symptoms which get the bulk of our attention. (75)

Rene Wadlow: "I agree, but there is a danger of thinking that all problems come from a single source (such as) sin. It can be so general an idea as to become nonoperational."

Rather than divine essence, Majid Rahnema would use "the wider transcendental world of which we are a part."

3. While dealing with the problems it is important to keep in mind certain realities that are often overlooked:

Women and Nature have been regarded as resources to be taken for granted, utilized and exploited. Feminine values play too small a role in international politics and economics. (89)

Measures taken nowadays to alleviate economic problems—tightening the money supply and risking recession on one hand, or loosening the money supply and risking inflation on the other hand—are simplistic and ineffective. (77)

Many learned skills (as well as the desire to help) are vital to effective citizen diplomacy. (69)

The UN has played a major role in shaping the evolution of humanity in the past 40 years. (61)

Caesar Voute: "It could have done better if the countries' governments had applied wiser policies."

Humanity's appropriate role in the overall scheme of things is *not* lord over Nature, but part of Nature. (76)

Hilkka Pietila: "(Rather,) a caretaker or caring steward of Nature."

Jan van der Linden agrees with Ms. Pietila: "We need to be a responsible and loving lord, not an arrogant one; but we are more than nature."

Howard Richards: "We need to change our social decision-making systems so that profit will no longer be the bottom line. A new self-perception needs to go with a new way to decide what actions to take."

4. Following are some vital steps to be taken toward healing the world:

The Third World needs to unite to present a force against exploitation. (61)

Archie Bahm: " . . . needs to unite with the rest of the world."

Caesar Voute agrees with Mr Bahm: "The First, Second and Third Worlds all need to cooperate."

John Fobes adds that there is a Third World "in every country that needs our attention and cooperation."

Mass education is vital. A generation aware of environmental problems will provide the needed momentum to correct them. (81)

Howard Richards: "Awareness of the problem does not equal understanding how to construct viable solutions."

We need worldwide education that teaches children love and respect for self, society and planet—a global education scheme that encompasses, our planet's relation to the universe, the human family, our place in time, and individual human life. (86)

We must foster self-realization, which provides a more powerful, more thoughtful incentive than profit in making and selling products and providing services. (69)

We should rearrange the economy in such a way that products of basic need are cheap and accessible. (65)

Caesar Voute: "Perhaps an overoptimistic statement about the possibilities of a planned economy."

Howard Richards: "This is the goal, not much help in itself for learning how to reach the goal. This could be done by encouraging local agriculture. To make a system of preference for local production of basic foods work, we need new attitudes and new laws."

We should make food staples a utility secured for everyone, not a standard commodity. (69)

Rene Wadlow: "The real question is how!"

Howard Richards: "To achieve this it is imperative to achieve spiritual discipline, without which we are compelled to rely on brutal discipline such as withholding access to food."

Caesar Voute: "Be careful; in may instances a market economy operates better than a planned economy, as demonstrated by Eastern Europe."

With today's global economy must come a new method of collaboration among the big groups (nations, religions, transnational corporations, etc.) based on cooperation and trust. (81)

Keith Suter agrees: "There has to be cooperation on common problems; An expanded concept of the common heritage of humankind is a good focal point for international cooperation."

Howard Richards: "Yes, but we also need to make a mosaic; plan for diversity, create smallness."

Majid Rhanema seems to like the idea but wonders: "How can it be made possible?"

Sustainable development (the satisfaction of everyone's basic needs and the growth and maintenance of society in a way that preserves environmental integrity) must become a policy and way of life in all countries and societies, as well as a guiding value in all minds and hearts. (91)

Majid Rhanema argues: "Sustainable development is a myth, or a contradiction in terms. For development, in all its forms, is a way of imposing an alien way of life on vernacular societies. As such, it cannot be sustainable."

We need to rebuild economics (or if that's impossible, replace it) with new tools such as futures research, game theory, cross-impact studies, systems theory, the Quality of Life Index and the Human Needs Index. (67)

Caesar Voute: "We can't replace it."

Competition and financial self-betterment are valuable until they become obsessive to the point where friendships and neighborhoods are strained at the personal and social levels, and where at the international level weapons proliferate, resources are pillaged and the plight of the Third World is ignored. Then it is time to come up with a plan to foster a sense of common heritage among these individuals and groups. (63)

> *Keith Suter adds: "The globe's environment is too important to be left to individual governments."*
>
> *Howard Richards: "Yes, but individual conversion needs to go hand in hand with structural transformation."*
>
> *Majid Rhanema is doubtful: "How can such an (inner) sense be fostered through an outer plan?"*
>
> *Hilkka Pietila is not convinced that competition is ever valuable.*
>
> *Joseph Schaeffer recommends "cooperative competition."*

Common heritage, the idea that certain areas are outside national control, is currently applied to the oceans, the moon and outer space. It should be broadened to apply also to forests, topsoil, the atmosphere and other portions of the global ecosystem whose destruction imperils our species and our future. (67)

> *Howard Richards: "We need to balance (the global heritage idea) with local control and local sense of place, building on the existing forms of trust in existing communities."*
>
> *Majid Rhanema: "It is the sense of the sacred and the realization of the fact that one is an integral part of a wider transcendental reality that can alone lead a subject to perceive the common heritage."*

Citizen diplomacy can be a valuable force in easing tensions among nations and groups if gone about appropriately. It can aggravate a situation if handled poorly. (61)

Citizen diplomats and offical (government) diplomats could be much more effective than they are today if they worked together. (59)

> *Chellis Glendinning: "As long as it doesn't water down citizens' efforts."*
>
> *Howard Richards: "My experience with US embassies abroad is that they mainly represent US business."*

In an era of growing communication, some existing incompatibilities are bound to be magnified and brought to the forefront. Learning the techniques of citizen diplomacy can alleviate the friction. (56)

To update or replace economics we need to identify the basic components of human economy. These are:

• Household production, cultivation of renewable resources, extraction of nonrenewable resources and processing of products. (63)

• The formal competitive market economy with its private and public sectors, the unpaid cooperative countereconomy, and Mother Nature which does her best to fulfill our desires and absorb our wastes. (58)

We need to analyze these components and we need methods and measures to bring these components into consideration in economic planning and policy-making. (69)

Howard Richards: "I would rather say that the very ideas—economics, planning, policy—are part of the problem."

As a last word, Majid Rahnema warns:

"In so-called modern times, designs aimed at changing or healing the world represent an invitation to political manipulators and unscrupulous professionals to find new ways of exercising their hegemony and control over others. As such, I have come to fear any design which might further diminish people's autonomy over their own lives. Solutions of a universal nature offered to preserve Mother Earth, to foster so-called mass education, to create united fronts against Third World exploitation, or to develop others have so far resulted mainly in reinforcing the positions of the individuals or corporate bodies responsible for the situation. Systems approaches, methodologies, or institutions which are proposed by both, are thus, often more dangerous than conducive to the promised results. Creative or right action emerges naturally as sensitive and compassionate minds learn to relate and to free themselves from different forms of conditioning."

Table 2: Healing Our Lives, Our Societies and Our Planet

Healing ourselves.

Leading-edge professionals in medicine, psychology, spirituality and other fields of human well-being acknowledge that true healing is an integrated process involving the complete person—body, mind, emotions and spirit. For an individual in need of healing the process includes:

Good nutrition. Taking into the body only wholesome things — not only good food, pure water and clean air, but wholesome news, movies, conversation and reading that will nourish the mind as well.

Healthy structure. Regular exercise to keep the cells and tissues fit. Massage and deep tissue manipulation to release toxins from tissues and help them realign to their natural state. When necessary, surgery to keep the body structurally sound and secure.

Balanced energy. Learning to bring one's chi, or life force, into balance, as through Qi Gong (meditation, movement and physical balancing).

A doctor's supportive attitude and tendency to provide careful guidance with the patient and to share knowledge freely, making healing a team effort.

A sense of control over our lives and our healing process. The realization that we cannot be idle bystanders while someone else heals us.

An attitude that our condition holds challenges to face, not problems to cope with. **A view of an exciting life,** not a gloomy one.

Open expression or communication of feelings.

Forgiveness as a prerequisite to peace of mind — forgiveness of people in our past who gave us emotional scars. Releasing resentments.

Mental imagery/meditation. Tuning into inner realities. Sensitizing ourself to the needs of our inner elements and to the guidance of a higher intelligence.

A sense that we are each an important part of society. A sense of **commitment to the whole.** We are part of society, not apart from it.

Deeply held knowledge of our personal nature.

A general sense of self-acceptance, self-love, and self-esteem that makes us glow and keeps us smiling.

A positive mental outlook toward treatment.

Coping well with stress, play and laughter, and exercise.

Healing our societies and planet.

Leading-edge professionals in government, economics, climatology and other world-spanning fields acknowledge that social and planetary healing must be an integrated process involving all people and groups. For a society or planet in need of healing the process must include:

Sensible, sustainable economics. Taking into the system only what can be extracted and used in a clean, wholesome fashion without depleting planetary resources or permanently damaging ecosystems.

Healthy social structures. Cleaning waterways, repairing buildings, communication and transportation networks, keeping neighborhoods neat, and other efforts to keep society structurally sound and secure.

Sensible energy policies in all societies based on renewable resources, with effective ways of distributing energy from its sources to its targets.

The UN's supportive, knowledgable assistance to nations, NGO's organizations, and other groups committed to healing the planet.

A sense of control over the destiny of our species and planet. A realization that we *will heal global ills.*

A general worldwide feeling that today's situation is a set of challenges to meet, not problems to suffer. **An exciting destiny**, not a gloomy one.

Open travel and communication across national borders.

Forgiveness as a prerequisite to world peace — forgiveness between cultures for past conflicts and atrocities that have left cultural scars.

A feedback policy for governments and the UN organization sensitizing them to the needs and concerns of the people, groups and ecosystems they represent. Accepting guidance by the UN.

A sense of planetary stewardship, the feeling that it is our destiny and responsibility to keep the ecosystems around us clean and healthy. A general worldwide feeling that we humans are an important part of Nature and the world, and not apart from it.

Widely held knowledge of our species and our world.

A general, worldwide love of the human species. An appreciation of our collective strengths and a commitment to bolster our weaknesses.

A general, worldwide **belief in a positive destiny** .

International sports and cultural activities.

There are parallels among life's levels — cells, individuals, communities . . . and planet. Unconditional love is the force that can blend them together.

—*MHM*

INDEX

About the Editor

Mark Macy is a native Coloradan. He gave up tobacco in the '70s and alcohol in the '80s. His wife, Regina, says he'd better be careful what he gives up in the '90s. Mark's background is in writing and journalism. It was on the mud-slinging campaign trail as a political press aide that it occurred to him there could be a better way of hiring our leaders and managing society. So he started collecting bits of wisdom that he hoped to keep alive in the overwhelming flood of information nowadays. His interests, besides writing, are music, meditation, exercise, forests and oceans, world affairs and travel. He lives with his wife and son, Aaron, in Greeley, Colorado.

Resources for Creative Change

To receive your copy of the **Guidebook for the '90s: Resources for Effecting Personal and Social Change** please write:

 Knowledge Systems, Inc.
7777 West Morris Street
Indianapolis, IN 46231

Call (317) 241-0749 or fax (317) 248-1503

We screen hundreds of publishers and networks for books, tapes and organizations to assist you in...

✔ coping with overload
✔ engaging in sacred play
✔ creating sacred time & space
✔ making sense of the times
✔ discovering high vocational adventure
✔ catalyzing creativity in organizations
✔ exploring the new consciousness
✔ and much, much more!